The Solo Singer in the Choral Setting

A Handbook for Achieving Vocal Health

Margaret Olson

THE SCARECROW PRESS, INC.
Lanham • Toronto • Plymouth, UK
2010

Published by Scarecrow Press, Inc.
A wholly owned subsidiary of The Rowman & Littlefield Publishing Group, Inc.
4501 Forbes Boulevard, Suite 200, Lanham, Maryland 20706
http://www.scarecrowpress.com

Estover Road, Plymouth PL6 7PY, United Kingdom

British Library Cataloguing in Publication Information Available

Library of Congress Cataloging-in-Publication Data

Olson, Margaret
  The solo singer in the choral setting : a handbook for achieving vocal health /
Margaret Olson.
    p. cm.
  ISBN 978-0-8108-7735-1 (hardcover : alk. paper) — ISBN 978-0-8108-6913-4 (pbk. :
alk. paper) — ISBN 978-0-8108-6914-1 (ebook)
  1. Choral singing—Instruction and study 2. Singing—Instruction and study. I. Title.
  MT875.O47 2010
  782.5'143—dc22   2010023681

Printed in the United States of America

Contents

~

Foreword

Ingo R. Titze, PhD

It was a pleasure to work with Margaret Olson on the original essay that was the inspiration for this book. Dealing with the solo voice in a choir is a non-trivial problem. Many technical aspects could be discussed at the outset, but to begin the exploration with comments and expressions from a broad spectrum of voice professionals is an excellent idea. I hope it makes interesting reading for many vocologists.

Preface

The purpose of this book is to present issues relevant to the solo singer in the choral setting and to offer practical solutions for resolving these issues. These solutions are intended to help teachers of singing, choral conductors, and singers successfully navigate the challenges of singing in a choral ensemble. This book most specifically addresses singers who are in the process of developing their vocal technique, and the challenges they face—physiological, pedagogical, psychological, interpretive, and acoustic—in both the choral and solo environment.

The book is intended for singers who participate in choir at the undergraduate or graduate level, as well as for professional, pre-professional, or amateur singers who are involved in a school, church, or community choir. The book can also be used as a text for choral conductors and conducting students, at the undergraduate and graduate level.

The topic of this book has been a great interest of mine for several years. During my doctoral work at the University of Iowa, I was required to participate in choral ensembles for two years and had the privilege of working with conductor Dr. Timothy Stalter. He created an environment in which I felt empowered to do my best work. His leadership and instruction fostered an extremely positive attitude in his singers, choral and solo alike, and allowed me to think creatively within the ensemble. It was in this environment that I started to seriously consider the topic of this book.

Participating in a choral ensemble at that stage of my vocal development was a useful and valuable learning experience. I was required to sing each day in rehearsal, thus keeping my instrument flexible, but there were other benefits. Singing under an ingenious conductor was an excellent opportunity to develop my understanding of the nuances of musicality. As a young teacher, I was able to closely observe how other singers produced sound and responded to verbal cues from the conductor. I was exposed to a variety of vocal literature and composers I had not encountered previously, and this knowledge influenced my repertoire selections as a soloist.

Throughout my choral experience, I found that the voice production required of me differed from the voice production I used in practice and in the studio. I do not wish to place a value judgment on this modification of my solo technique, but beyond a doubt, it was required for choral participation. Is this a positive or a negative? I will not answer that question categorically in this book, but the experience did cause me to think deeply about the differences between the art forms of solo and choral singing. I searched for sources that would help me navigate this dual experience while meeting the many vocal demands of my degree.

While pursuing the Doctor of Musical Arts degree, in any given semester I was usually preparing a sixty-minute solo recital while attending classes where I was expected to sing arias or art songs. In addition, I had daily practice, weekly voice lessons, and studio class. An additional strain on my voice was the teaching of fifteen to eighteen private students each week. These demands are not unusual for any graduate vocal student, but they are greatly taxing on the voice. When I sought the advice of fellow students, or even professors, the general response was that we should all "just do the best we can."

I never discovered any book to help me. The available literature on the topic of the solo singer in the choral setting imparted various scientific facts and opinions of music professionals, but included little in the way of conclusive scientific studies, statistical research data, or practical advice. I have not undertaken a statistical data-gathering study here, but hopefully this book will attract the attention of other voice professionals and result in further research.

I did find an excellent master's thesis, however: *The Effect of Choral Singing on the Developing Solo Voice*, written by James Luther Wrolstad in 1979 while he was at California State University, Fullerton. Wrolstad's thesis excited me as a singer and inspired me to continue researching this topic. The thesis stands out as a pivotal work for two reasons: first, it was one of the earliest sources to address the central theme of this book; and second, it quotes singers and choral conductors alike on the issues surrounding the solo singer in the choral setting.

While not every teacher or conductor will agree with all of the ideas presented in this book, the proposals are offered in a straightforward manner geared toward promoting the health of the singer and fostering dialogue among singer, teacher, and choral conductor. The time has come for solo singers to embrace the challenge of singing healthfully in choral ensembles, and for teachers of singing and conductors to communicate freely about the real issues these singers face.

It is my hope that this book will make a positive contribution to both solo and choral singing, and that it will begin a new era of understanding and communication among singers, teachers of singing, and choral conductors.

~

Acknowledgments

I would like to thank my editor, Renée Camus, and all of the individuals at Scarecrow Press for the opportunity to work on this project. I would like to thank Elizabeth S. Olson, M.A., Sherry Frank, project management professional, and Stephanie Ward, Esq., for editing my manuscript.

I would like to offer a special thank you to Martha Randall for her time and invaluable assistance. I am also extremely appreciative of Dr. Carroll Gonzo for giving his time and wise input so generously.

Thank you to Dr. Ingo Titze (tenor!) for writing the foreword of this book, and also for his integrity, generosity, and unlimited contributions to voice science and singers. Thank you to Dr. Hugh Ferguson Floyd for his excellent contributions to my manuscript and for his assistance.

Thanks so much to Dr. Melinda O'Neal and Dr. Timothy Stalter for sharing their great knowledge in the two interviews included in the appendix.

Thank you to University of Iowa faculty Dr. Katherine Eberle, Susan Sondrol Jones, Rachel Joselson, and Stephen Swanson. Thank you to Morgan State University faculty Dr. Stephanie Bruning, Shirley Basfield-Dunlap, and Milton Aldana. Thank you also to Dr. John Nix and Margaret Baroody.

A sincere thank you to Dr. Richard Sjoerdsma for his support and leadership over the years. Thanks to Tadd Russo for formatting the *vocalises* and musical examples.

I would also like to offer special thanks and great appreciation to three choral conductors and musical mentors: Joel Adams, Dr. William P. Carroll, and Dr. Timothy Stalter. (I really hope you like the book!)

Finally, thank you to Marilynn and Michael Olson for their support, and to my family and friends.

Introduction

Choral singing and solo singing, while related, are distinct art forms. Both utilize the human voice as the primary instrument, but in entirely different ways. One is not better than the other, just different. Yet because of unique demands on the voice in each environment, this topic has aroused some controversy among choral conductors and teachers of singing.

The choral conductor Dr. Robert Fountain agrees that solo singing and choral singing pose distinct challenges:

> I think solo singing is an art in itself. One baritone solo-singing art songs, singing Schubert art songs, is certainly different from a bass section singing *B minor Mass*. Choral singing is a group effort, involving group dynamics. It is a group of people working for something that one of them really cannot do alone. Whereas on the other hand, the solo singer is doing something that a group cannot do.[1]

Not much scientific research has clarified how the voice is used in a group as opposed to a solo environment. Studies have measured differences in pitch quality, intonation, intensity, and acoustic load, but without reaching indisputable conclusions. For example, in a 2007 study named "The Acoustic Characteristics of Professional Opera Singers Performing in Chorus Versus Solo Mode,"[2] researchers used head-mounted microphones to examine individual singers' peak energy while singing different vowels; however, the subjects were in an operatic, not choral, ensemble.

As voice science becomes more sophisticated and more data is collected and analyzed, the differences between solo and choral singing will gain more factual support. Meanwhile, singers must navigate both art forms while maintaining vocal health and longevity.

Singers have traditionally modified their vocal technique to fully participate in the choral ensemble, to the dismay of some teachers of singing. Similarly, some solo singers and teachers have disregarded the value of choral singing, to the dismay of choral conductors. One purpose of this book is to examine and dispel some of these issues, in order to increase tolerance among members of the music community. In the words of the late Richard Miller: "There is a history of conflict in American academic circles between the training of the solo voice and what is expected of a singer in the choral ensemble. Such conflict need not exist."[3]

In today's university or collegiate setting, undergraduate vocal majors usually find themselves singing regularly in more than one environment and balancing ensemble participation with solo study and performance demands. Students may also have an opera-oriented class and singing commitments outside of school. A voice major may spend up to twelve hours a week singing inside and outside of class, excluding private practice time. Many voice teachers recommend two hours a day for personal practice, which can bring the total to twenty-two hours of singing a week. Such a schedule is quite demanding for a young singer whose technique may not be firmly established and polished.[4]

University students are not the only individuals facing challenges in the choral environment. Amateur singers are an integral and critical part of music making across the United States. They are the voices in community, symphonic, *a cappella*, chamber, and church choirs of all kinds. If not for the tireless commitment and effort of these amateur singers, choral music could hardly sustain itself as an art form. These singers were often music majors in college, or had some other voice training, but pursued another career. Many studied voice privately and maintain an avid interest in vocal pedagogy and healthy singing. Amateur singers can benefit as much as professionals from heightened awareness and a proactive pedagogical approach to the choral ensemble.

There are many benefits to participating in a choral ensemble. Exposure to the choral works of major composers gives the individual a broader context and greater understanding of each composer's musical style. This understanding can then be applied to the same composer's solo literature. For example, singing Brahms's *Zigeunerlieder* (Op. 103) in a choral environment can only enhance a solo singer's inherent understanding of Brahms's unique rhythms and complex harmonies. Exposure to choral literature can also alert singers to the many solo opportunities within choral works. These solos are perfect opportunities for singers to use their solo skills while also participating as members of the ensemble.

In the choral environment, the solo singer can also gain an understanding of how to work with and follow a conductor, skills which can be applied to opera, oratorio, and concert work. Singers in a choral ensemble can consider whether to pursue choral conducting or choral singing professionally, while observing both disciplines as a participant.

On a technical level, choir can help soloists gain practical ensemble experience for future use as singers or teachers; improve musical skills, sight-reading, and part-reading; and keep the voice in good shape through regular usage. For many individuals, choral singing is a fun group activity that brings great satisfaction and enjoyment.

The solo singer should be aware that many professional opera singers laud the benefits of choral singing and have themselves participated in choirs professionally, while pursuing outstanding solo careers. These singers include Thomas Hampson, Samuel Ramey, and Ruth Ann Swenson.[5] However, Hampson feels that while choral ensembles offer well-rounded training, the soloist will eventually need to depart:

> I think the biggest problem for a solo professional singer in a choir is homogeneous sound. Choral singing demands a melding and listening, which as a discipline is fantastic. It can, however, for a real solo voice, be detrimental at some point. . . . Each individual needs to determine the correct time to pursue solo work exclusively.[6]

There are as many opinions on the subject of solo versus choral singing as there are singers! Singer Donald Hoiness compares singers with concert pianists to argue against the group approach: "I do not think there is any more logic in trying to develop a real singer in a collective manner than there is in the case of gifted pianists."[7] There is a certain amount of logic here: a concert pianist is not trained to play within a group of people, and similarly, a solo singer is trained to display the voice individually. On the other hand, there is a plethora of choral literature, but very little music written for multiple pianos.

One should consider that most singers do not earn a living as soloists, but through a combination of choral and solo work. Therefore, it is imperative that solo singers in training learn to use their voices successfully in the choral environment. For most singers pursuing a solo career, the choral ensemble will be a realistic part of their musical path in one way or another.

If voice teachers take a dispassionate and clear-eyed view of the pool of students they have worked with over their careers, most probably would agree that very few of their students encompassed the skill levels necessary to achieve careers as solo singers. For most voice students, particularly in a secondary educational system of any kind in the United States, the choral experience should be relevant and substantial to their musical study and growth.

If voice teachers and choral conductors can freely admit that solo and choral singing are distinct and separate art forms—and concurrently, that these art forms are very similar—an amicable discussion can take place about the real differences between them, and the challenges that each presents to young singers.

While most singers and vocal majors can benefit from choral experience, there is no doubt that some voices do not belong in a choral ensemble. Some singers possess voices of prodigious size that are truly outside the norm. Others may have a vocal deficiency, such as a vibrato rate that is excessively fast or slow and cannot be easily altered. A singer may possess a truly unique timbre that cannot be modified to fit within a section of the ensemble. An increasingly common reason for a *male* singer not to participate in choir is that he is pursuing some type of countertenor technique (utilizing the unique male *falsetto* register), and in the early stages of his study he cannot make the modifications required in the choral ensemble. Finally, students returning to school after performing as professional singers may not be able to alter their technique to fit into an ensemble; the muscle memory required for solo singing may be too firmly ingrained.

Perhaps the most common reason some teachers want to keep an extraordinary student out of the choral ensemble is that the student has the true potential for a solo career. Most teachers of singing come across very few students of this caliber, but when they do, it may be obvious that the student's voice is a truly phenomenal instrument that should not be utilized in a choral ensemble. Why? A fundamental requirement for a choral voice is that it can be indistinguishable from other voices, or "blended," to function as part of a group. Some special voices are most appropriately utilized on the operatic stage. It may be in the best interest of these students to focus solely on solo technique and repertoire while in the academic environment.

Voice teachers should weigh the benefits and usefulness of placing a young singer with potential for a solo career in a choral ensemble. Voice teacher Donald Hoiness argues for steering such students away from choral ensembles:

In my opinion, young people with the potential of being singers, in the finest sense of that word, should stay far away from intense and prolonged involvement in the choral ensemble. A young singer of potential should be consumed in the business of training his or her individual voice without having to submerge himself in the sounds and habits of other singers, without having to be part of the scheme of a director to do his own thing, and without having to contribute so much to the public relations department of a college. Choral experience is irrelevant for the process of becoming a solo singer.[8]

Some conservatory vocal programs geared toward the solo performer, such as the Juilliard School and the Curtis Institute of Music, do not include choral singing as a requirement in the undergraduate curriculum, because their programs are focused on training the solo voice.[9]

Once again, if singers, teachers, and conductors can agree that the art forms of solo and choral singing are distinct and require different techniques, then Hoiness's statement comes across as less provocative.

Some choral conductors may agree that a singer who is totally focused on solo singing or opera as a career will not ultimately benefit from prolonged time in the choral ensemble. Pursuing an operatic career is a consuming endeavor and the demands of the repertoire require complete focus. Likewise, voice teachers may feel that students intent on careers as professional choral singers should avoid enrolling in opera workshop every semester, and focus primarily on choral literature and experience. Some students can do both, but vocal and choral majors will not consider both art forms identical, nor should they. Age, experience, and career goals should also be taken into consideration.

Each chapter of this book explores specific issues relating to the solo singer in the choral setting, and includes proposed solutions for the solo singer, teacher of singing, and choral conductor.

Chapter one is an overview of the mechanics of voice production. The rest of the chapters address specific physiological, pedagogical, psychological, interpretive, and acoustic issues. Chapter two addresses the physiological issues of age, challenging *tessituras*, singing by sensation (rather than sound), independence from instruction, the nontraditional student, and posture. Chapter three examines pedagogical issues relating to warm-ups, resonation, individual timbre, respiration, intonation, and the special case of the amateur choral singer. The chapter also offers the singer tips for maintaining intonation in choir.

Chapter four discusses issues relating to vibrato in the choral ensemble, with special attention paid to the adult and aging singer. Non-vibrato singing, sometimes referred to as "straight tone," is a challenging issue for solo singers and is addressed in detail.

The choral approach to diction, including the articulation of vowels and consonants, is considered in chapter five. Chapter six examines specific choral issues such as voice classification, choral blend, demands of the choral rehearsal, and the tone quality expectations of the conductor.

Chapter seven reviews psychological issues, such as the relationship among choral conductor, teacher of singing, and student; the solo-versus-choral mind-set; and the question of what singers want from choral conductors. The emphasis is on relationships, with many tips for all parties involved in choral singing.

Chapter eight addresses issues of interpretation, from expressing emotion through the voice to the integration of music and drama in choral performance. Specific techniques for analyzing and interpreting choral texts are provided.

Chapter nine examines acoustic issues: listening to others, feedback and reference, the Lombard effect, and the singers' formant in the choral ensemble. Specific *vocalises* for the choral ensemble are presented in chapter ten, with each principal category of vocalization covered.

The appendix contains an interview with two scholars who are choral conductors. The questions pertain to the topics addressed in the book, and the responses are unedited and candid, offering readers additional perspectives. A complete glossary is included at the end of the text.

Some sections present a teaching case study that examines a particular vocal issue frequently encountered by students and their teachers. These case studies are based on actual situations, but the names of students have been changed to maintain their anonymity.

In order to codify the musical examples, the following abbreviations are used: mm for measure, m for minor, and M for major. A letter followed by a number refers to the octave of the pitch as it relates to the keyboard; for example, C4 refers to middle C, C5 is an octave above middle C, and G5 is a fifth above C5. "Fifth," "fourth," "third," and so on refer to intervals.

The following terms are choral classifications beginning with the lowest male voice part and ending with the highest female voice part: Bass II, Bass I (F2 to F4); Tenor II, Tenor I (D3 to B4); Alto II, Alto I (A3 to G5); and Soprano II, Soprano I (B3 to B5). Foreign language terms are *italicized* in the text, and definitions are available in the glossary, if needed.

If we, as musicians and members of academic communities, can acknowledge that our solo and choral art forms are distinct from one another, yet closely related, we can begin an honest and worthwhile discussion of the issues. This book begins that discussion. With awareness and a better understanding of how to use one's voice in a group setting, the singer is more likely to achieve success and vocal health both within the choral ensemble and onstage as a solo singer.

Notes

1. Quoted in James Luther Wrolstad, "The Effect of Choral Singing on the Developing Solo Voice" (master's thesis, California State University, Fullerton, 1979), 123.

2. Katherine L. P. Reid, Pamela Davis, Jennifer Oates, Densil Cabera, Sten Ternström, Michael Black, and Janice Chapman, "The Acoustic Characteristics of Professional Opera Singers Performing in Chorus Versus Solo Mode," *Journal of Voice* 21 (2007): 35–45.

3. Richard Miller, "The Solo Singer in the Choral Ensemble," *Choral Journal* 36 (1995): 31.

4. Barbara M. Doscher, *The Functional Unity of the Singing Voice* (London: The Scarecrow Press, 1994), 241.

5. Randi Von Ellefson, "An Opera Soloist Reflects on Choral Singing: An Interview with Thomas Hampson," *Choral Journal* 37 (1996): 37–39.

6. Von Ellefson, "An Opera Soloist Reflects," 37–39.

7. Quoted in Wrolstad, "The Effect of Choral Singing," 51.

8. Quoted in Wrolstad, "The Effect of Choral Singing," 145–46.

9. For degree requirements at these institutions, see their websites www.juilliard.edu/college and www.curtis.edu.

CHAPTER ONE

~

Overview of Voice Production

Voice teachers and choral conductors are well-versed in voice production, but recreational singers as well as students of singing and conducting may benefit from a review of the singing instrument and its functions. This chapter provides a basic description of the voice production used in singing, so that readers will be able to follow the many aspects of vocal technique and voice science discussed in this book.

The following is an overview only, and readers should seek out additional texts, as well as a good voice teacher, for more detailed information. The bibliography at the conclusion of the book lists several written resources.

Structure

The voice has three special characteristics that distinguish it from any other musical instrument: it is carried within the human body; it cannot be seen by the human eye; and it performs a biological as well as musical function.

The voice itself is actually a structure within the neck known as the larynx, or "voice box." The larynx,[1] situated at the top of the trachea (windpipe), is made of cartilages and connected to a bone known as the hyoid bone. The hyoid bone, commonly known as the "lone bone," is located at the base of the tongue and the top of the larynx, and has the distinction of being the only bone in the human body that is not attached to another bone. These structures form the framework of the larynx.

Downward from the hyoid bone is the thyroid cartilage (plate-like, with the "Adam's apple" in front) and the cricoid cartilage (ring-shaped), with the arytenoid cartilages (triangular) attached. The epiglottis is hinged onto the thyroid cartilage and functions as a lid for the larynx. The biological purpose of the epiglottis is to protect the airway from food and liquids during swallowing. It is useful to think of the Greek origins of these cartilage names when considering their orientation and shape; for example, "ring" for cricoid, "shield" for thyroid, and "ladles" for arytenoids.[2]

In addition to cartilages, the larynx also contains ligaments, membranes, and muscles. For the purposes of this review, we will focus only on the muscles. The muscles of the larynx control the vocal folds, also known as vocal cords. These muscles can adduct the vocal folds (bring them together, to make them thicker and shorter) or abduct them (move them apart, to make them longer and thinner).

Muscles of the voice are divided into two categories: intrinsic muscles have both ends connected within the larynx, while extrinsic muscles have one end within the larynx and one end outside the larynx. The intrinsic muscles of the larynx are: the thyroarytenoid muscle (also known as the *vocalis* or vocal folds), the principle muscle of phonation; the cricothyroid muscle, the pitch-changing muscle that with an increase of tension makes the folds lengthen; and the cricoarytenoid and interarytenoid muscles.

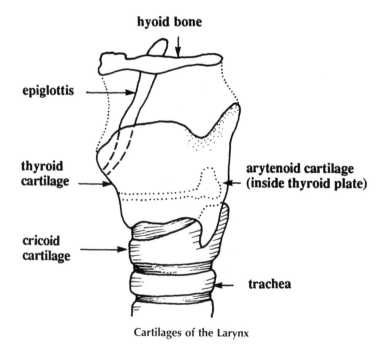

hyoid bone

epiglottis

thyroid cartilage

arytenoid cartilage (inside thyroid plate)

cricoid cartilage

trachea

Cartilages of the Larynx

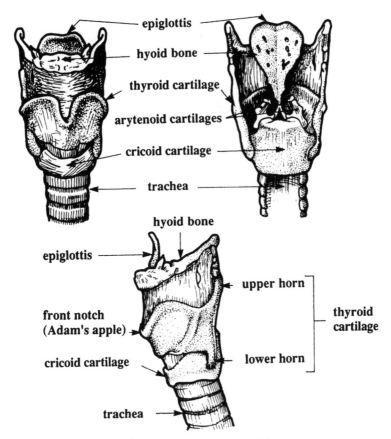

epiglottis

hyoid bone

thyroid cartilage

arytenoid cartilages

cricoid cartilage

trachea

hyoid bone

epiglottis

upper horn

front notch
(Adam's apple)

thyroid
cartilage

cricoid cartilage

lower horn

trachea

Alternative Views of the Cartilages of the Larynx[3]

Extrinsic muscles of the larynx are divided into two categories: the suprahyoids, which raise the larynx, and the infrahyoids, which lower the larynx. The suprahyoids include the digastric muscle, the stylohyoid muscle, the mylohyoid muscle, the geniohyoid muscle, and the hyoglossus muscle. The infrahyoids include the sternohyoid muscle, the sternothyroid muscle, the omohyoid muscle, and the thyrohyoid muscle.[4]

These muscles, cartilages, membranes, and ligaments, along with the hyoid bone, form the laryngeal mechanism. However, the structure of the vocal instrument is not limited to the laryngeal area. The entire human body is involved in the process of singing. The framework of the vocal instrument is also the framework of the body. The spinal column, sternum, scapula, and clavicles support the weight of the body, and the rib cage and pelvis provide shelter for vital organs. In singing, the larynx is dependent on the healthy framework of the body.

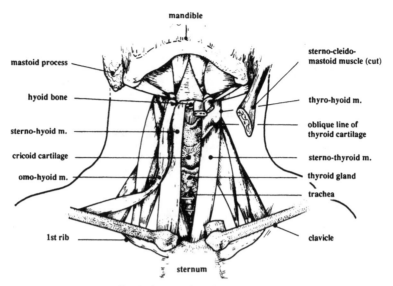

Extrinsic Muscles of the Larynx

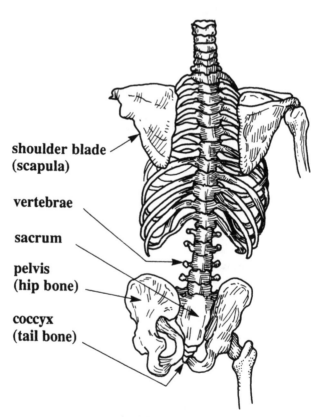

Framework of the Skeletal Structure

Respiration

To breathe properly while singing, good posture is necessary. Much has been written on this topic, but perhaps Richard Miller said it best when he described proper posture as "noble."[5] This is a great way to describe correct posture to students, since the word "noble" evokes a positive attitude rather than a boring description of anatomy!

What exactly constitutes this "noble" posture? In a standing position, the spine should be straight and tall but not stiff. The feet should be about a foot apart, and the knees should not be locked. The sternum should be lifted, but not overly raised. Together these elements should allow the rib cage to fully expand and retract, achieving the optimum air exchange for the singer.

There is great interest in how breathing for singing is different than the involuntary breathing we do every day. The biggest difference is that in singing, the breathing process is very consciously controlled, while in daily activities, the breathing process is unconsciously executed.

There are basically four stages of the breath cycle: inhalation, suspension, exhalation, and recovery. The inhalation for singing should be silent. Silence during inhalation indicates that the vocal folds are open and ready for adduction. A gasping or noisy sound during inhalation (or inspiration) indicates that the vocal folds are prematurely somewhat adducted, which can signal tension and dry out the vocal folds. The principal muscles of respiration are the intercostal muscles between the ribs. The external intercostal muscles make inspiration possible by moving the rib cage outward and upward.

The diaphragm is a large, dome-shaped muscle at the base of the rib cage that flattens out during inhalation and returns to a resting position during exhalation. As the rib cage opens up and the diaphragm lowers, intercostal muscles stretch the lungs and create a vacuum effect, drawing air into the body. The lowering of the diaphragm shifts the *viscera* (internal organs), resulting in a slight expansion of the abdominal and epigastric (upper abdominal) regions.

The area of the body from the neck to the diaphragm is the thorax. Below the thorax is the diaphragm, which separates the thorax from the abdominal area. Even though the thorax and abdominal areas are distinct, they work together during respiration. Air comes through the nose and mouth, through the vocal tract, past the larynx, through the trachea, into the bronchi (air passageways made of cartilage that branch out from the trachea), and finally into the lungs.

The suspension phase of the breath cycle is the brief time between the inspiration and the start of the sung phrase. It should not be noticeable to

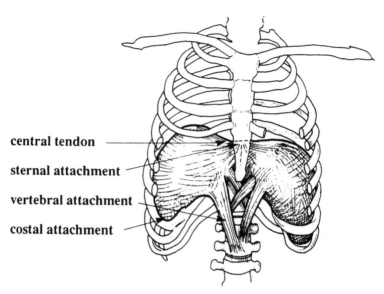

central tendon
sternal attachment
vertebral attachment
costal attachment

Front View of the Diaphragm

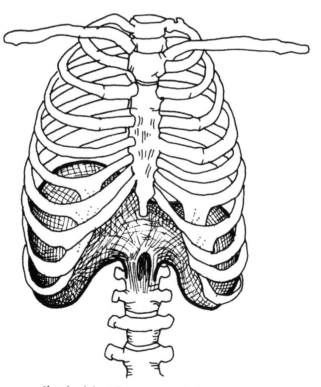

Sketch of the Rib Cage and Diaphragm at Rest

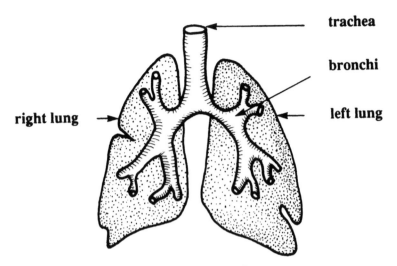

Sketch of the Lungs and Surrounding Structures

anyone but the singer. At the suspension phase, most singers engage their abdominal muscles as the support for the breath and tone. These muscles include the rectus sheath, the rectus abdominis, the external and internal obliques, and the transversus abdominis.[6]

The exhalation phase occurs when the musical phrase is sung. As an intrinsic part of phonation, breath is incorporated in the tone produced. The pace of air leaving the lungs depends on the demands of the phrase, the *tessitura* (pitch range), and the singer's technique. During this phase, the internal intercostal muscles return the rib cage to its original position, and the diaphragm slowly returns to its neutral position. In an ideal situation, the singer keeps the abdominal muscles engaged until the end of the sung phrase, while maintaining a feeling of fullness and expansion to the side and front of the rib cage area. In other words, the breath should not move out too quickly, the ribs should not collapse, and the abdominal muscles should not release at the beginning of the sung phrase.

The final stage of the breath cycle, the recovery phase, is an indicator of how the next sung phrase will sound. The singer should experience a sense of yielding and release of abdominal and laryngeal musculature before beginning the next inhalation. The length of the recovery phase depends solely on the composer's demands for the given repertoire.

Throughout the entire breath cycle the upper chest area, shoulders, neck, and head should remain still. The action of breathing takes place within the thoracic cage and below.

This description of the breath cycle summarizes how the breath should be managed—now a word about the term "breath support," which often has a more precise meaning than "breath management." The idea of breath support relates to the entire balance of musculature used throughout the breath cycle, but most specifically to the phase of exhalation when singing takes place.

The concept of "support" means different things to different singers. Some individuals may sense a "gripping" or "tightening" of musculature as support. While the abdominal muscles are engaged, however, the general goal is to keep airflow going and not to become rigid.

A concept of the historic Italian school of singing, *appoggio*, is closely related to "breath support" but less commonly referred to. *Appoggio*, from the verb *appoggiarsi* ("to lean upon"), has been described as "a system for combining and balancing muscles and organs of the trunk and neck, controlling their relationships to the supraglottal resonators, so that no exaggerated function of any one of them upsets the whole."[7] Proper *appoggio* technique not only balances the muscles used in singing, but also involves a distinct approach to the abdominal muscles, which should be "engaged" or "activated" rather than "pushed out" or "clenched." The engagement of the abdominal musculature should balance the engagement of the neck muscles, allowing for release, optimizing the resonance of the tone, and providing "support" for the sung phrase.

The mechanics of *appoggio* are highly detailed but essential to vocal coordination:

> In *appoggio* technique, the sternum must initially find a moderately high position; this position is then retained throughout the inhalation-exhalation cycle. Shoulders are relaxed, but the sternum never slumps. Because the ribs are attached to the sternum, sternal posture in part determines diaphragmatic position. If the sternum lowers, the ribs cannot maintain an expanded position, and the diaphragm must ascend more rapidly. Both the epigastric and umbilical regions should be stabilized so that a feeling of internal-external muscular balance is present. This sensation directly influences the diaphragm.[8]

Learning to balance the muscles of the neck, rib, and abdominal areas during inhalation, the sung phrase, and recovery is indispensable for any singer.

Phonation

Phonation is the act of producing sound. Both speech and singing are acts of phonation. In phonation the sound originates from the larynx, or more specifically, the vocal folds. The movement of air between the folds causes them to vibrate, and the result is vocal sound.

Prior to phonation, air pressure builds up underneath the vocal folds. This is known as subglottal pressure (the space between the vocal folds is called the *glottis*). The laryngeal muscles of adduction bring the folds together, while the subglottal pressure creates a vacuum effect, suctioning air between the folds to begin the vibration. Ideally, the breath and musculature of the larynx are in sync when the singer makes an attack or onset.

Qualities of a well-produced tone can be subjective. However, a freely produced tone with an even vibrato rate and resonance is preferred. In phonation singers should avoid hyperfunction (oversinging) and hypofunction (undersinging), as neither will result in the best possible sound.

Resonance

Resonance is basically the ringing of the voice. Resonance is what characterizes an individual singer's vocal timbre or tone. The voice is at its best when resonance is most present. Resonance is an extension of the singer's physiological makeup, and creates the color, nuance, and personality of the voice.

The question of exactly where resonation takes place is often discussed among voice teachers, scientists, and vocologists. The concepts presented here are generally agreed upon among professionals in the field.

The principal resonator of the vocal instrument is the *vocal tract*. The vocal tract, or tube, consists of the air spaces from the vocal folds to the lips. The pharyngeal section of the vocal tract lies between the top of the larynx and the rear of the mouth. The oral section is inside the mouth, and the nasal section is behind the nasal cavity. When the soft palate (the back roof of the mouth and top of the throat) is lowered, the nasal passages also become part of the vocal tract. Within the vocal tract are the articulators, some of which can move. The hard palate (the middle and front roof of the mouth) is stabilized and does not move, but can reflect sound. The soft palate can be manipulated, as well as the jaw and tongue. The lips are very flexible and essential to the shaping of tone. These articulators work together to shape the vocal tract resonator that begins at the larynx. The vocal tract resonator *produces* resonance. The shape of this resonator determines the vocal colors that we interpret as vowels, and additional sounds produce the consonants, so that words can be understood.

The shape and size of the vocal tract are unique to every individual. Some theories hold that a person with a more spacious vocal tract has

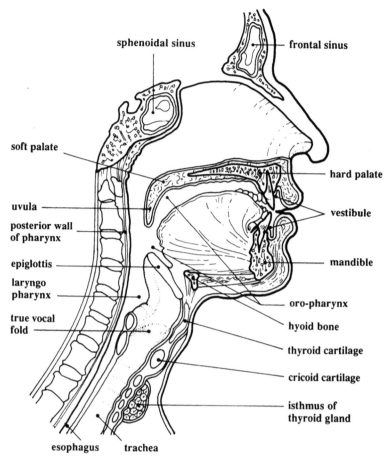

sphenoidal sinus — frontal sinus

soft palate

hard palate

uvula

vestibule

posterior wall of pharynx

epiglottis

mandible

laryngo pharynx

oro-pharynx

true vocal fold

hyoid bone

thyroid cartilage

cricoid cartilage

isthmus of thyroid gland

esophagus   trachea

The Vocal Tract and Surrounding Structures

deeper resonances, and even a larger-sized voice, but teachers of singing know this is not always true.

Since the voice is unique among instruments, there is a special name for vocal resonances: *formants*. A voice with a ringing tone is said to have the *singers' formant*. Singers often discuss how to manipulate and maximize resonance when performing or singing with an orchestra. Much has been written on the acoustic science of resonance if the reader is interested.[9]

How does the singer really sense, or *feel*, resonance? Singers and teachers generally agree that it is desirable to feel resonance forward in the face. Singers describe the sensation of resonance in the forehead, the mask of the face, the nasal area, the sinuses, the upper lip, and many other places. The idea of resonance vibrations in the head and chest (also known as bone conduction) is also accepted, although not all singers experience it in a similar manner.

A singer's sensation of resonance is directly related to the concept of voice placement. From voice science we have learned that it is not actually possible to "place" the voice. Once the tone is initiated within the larynx, all a singer can control is the shape of the vocal tract and the formation of the articulators.

Many teachers of singing use locational imagery in voice teaching. For example, in order to direct resonance, a teacher might tell a student to "feel the voice coming out of the top of the head like a whale's spout." This type of direction may or may not result in an improved sound from the singer. In another example, if a student needs to move a darkened vowel forward, a teacher might advise the student to "place the voice toward the hard palate, behind the front teeth." Of course technically there is nothing to actually "place," but a sense of forward energy may get the desired result. While the use of locational imagery in voice teaching remains somewhat controversial, teachers are advised to temper imagery with voice science to achieve the best possible result for the student.

Another concept related to resonance is the repositioning of the larynx. Much attention has been paid to the idea of "lowering the larynx," especially among tenors. Some singers believe that lowering the larynx will increase their resonance by lengthening the vocal tract. Many teachers of singing believe that the ideal position for the larynx in singing is similar to its resting position. This issue will continue to be debated among teachers of singing and voice scientists.

Registration

A vocal register is a series of pitches that share a uniform sound quality. Manuel Garcia II, a singer and pioneer vocal pedagogue, further defines the word "register":

> By the word register is to be understood a series of consecutive and homogenous sounds produced by the same mechanical means and differing essentially from other sounds originating in mechanical means of a different kind; hence it follows, that all the sounds belonging to the same register are of the same quality and nature, however great the modifications of quality and power they may undergo.[10]

The exact number of registers in the male and female voice is debatable. It is generally accepted that the female voice has three registers: the head, the middle, and the chest. The male voice generally has two registers, the head and chest, but it is perfectly acceptable to speak of a male middle register.

Additional register designations include the *flageolet* (or whistle register), which exists above the head voice in the female voice. The *strohbass* (or straw bass) register exists below the male chest voice, and is similar to the *vocal fry* register. (Vocal fry is not typically employed in singing; the sound is low and creaky, with an interrupted airflow.) The male voice also has the *falsetto* register.

The term falsetto describes the register above the head register in the male voice. Most male singers can access this register fairly easily, and some even use it for vocalizing or "marking" in rehearsal. Other men choose to develop the falsetto exclusively as professional countertenors. The timbre of the falsetto register is unique to every singer, and can be quite brilliant or thin and breathy. The last twenty years have seen many extraordinary countertenors enter the singing world, and modern countertenors are starting to have as much variety as any other vocal category.

Singers experience a unique transition event known as the *passaggio* (passage) when moving between registers. A *passaggio* occurs after a series of pitches that are similar in quality. A singer usually experiences a first and second *passaggio* point (*primo passaggio* and *secondo passaggio*), which differ for each voice type. For example, most tenors experience the primo *passaggio* around the same pitches. The same holds for mezzo-sopranos, sopranos, and basses, with adjustments made for range. A good teacher will probably not spend a lot of time discussing registers and transition points with students, but rather work toward unifying the registers through conscientious and careful vocalization in the lesson.

Voice classification, the process of placing a voice into the proper category, is directly related to registration. The process of classifying a voice is different for solo singing than for choral singing, though the vocal attributes that determine each classification are similar. These attributes for classifying a voice include timbre, range, tessitura, and sometimes the transition points between registers. In the solo singing genre of opera, body type, acting ability, and special vocal traits such as voice size and stamina are also considered.

In choral singing, the conductor may consider sight-reading ability and voice size when classifying a voice. Singers may be placed in a certain section because of their sight-reading skills, or to vocally improve a certain section. This may present a danger to solo singers, as it is essential for singers to use their instrument within the proper classification for optimal vocal health. Most voices are in the medium range, and the potential for vocal damage seems more prevalent in too high or too low a classification.[11]

In the choral ensemble, voices are generally classified as soprano, alto, tenor, or bass, with each part divided among two or three groups if needed. In opera, there are additional classifications for each voice type. For example, the soprano voice can be a *coloratura*, light lyric, *soubrette*, full lyric, dramatic, or *spinto* soprano. Variations are found in the mezzo-soprano, tenor, and bass categories as well. Traditionally, opera classifications are based on the *fach* system, which originated in Germany and matches opera roles to specific voice types. Most solo singers have committed to a fach by their late twenties, although some have not, and some switch fach categories because of physical changes or misclassification.

Misclassification of the voice can be dangerous for a singer, whether in a choral ensemble or a solo setting. Singers should work closely with a good teacher to avoid vocal damage and overuse.

Coordination

Beyond question, a good vocal technique requires coordination of tone, breath, and support. Vocal technique, and the coordination of all its parts, must be internalized through regular and conscientious practice by the singer. In *Singing: The First Art*, Dan Marek writes:

> The coordination . . . of the vocal cords becomes a major goal in the training of fine singers. The resulting tone, which is functionally balanced, is said to have *squillo*, or a "ring." The ability to control the interrelationship of the breath and the tensing function is one of the hallmarks of great singers. One thinks of the finesse and power of such artists as Adelina Patti, Enrico Caruso, Rosa Ponselle, and Jussi Björling. All were able to sing the softest tones without losing clarity and to swell smoothly to *fortissimo* and back again. This takes a miracle of coordination.[12]

Richard Miller spoke often of the various stages of vocalizing that should make up the practice regimen. These stages consist of onset exercises, resonance exercises, agility exercises, vowel differentiation exercises, *sostenuto* exercises, range extension exercises, and exercises of dynamic control. Singers who cover each of these stages daily are well on the way to a healthy voice! Regular use and practice of these concepts will reinforce coordination for all singers, from beginners to professionals.

One of the great mysteries of singing is how each singer finds the coordination of his instrument on his own. Coordination is not a concept that can be completely taught by another person. Learning to manage all aspects of singing in a balanced manner is an exciting journey for every singer, and can be achieved through a combination of individual practice and voice lessons. As William Vennard writes:

> The one thing that all must achieve is coordination. This is what every teacher works for in his studio. . . . Studio time should not be spent in academic discussion unless it leads to practical results. The student can learn as much as he likes from books, and can check his knowledge by questioning the teacher, but the main purpose of the lesson time is to practice the coordination of the vocal act.[13]

Vocal Health for Singers

Vocal health for singers is as complex as the health of any other system of the human body. How a singer feels is a primary indicator of how a singer will sing. For those who sing on a regular basis, common sense in regard to heath is imperative.

Singers should not overextend their voices in singing or in other situations. Caution should be employed in a noisy restaurant or crowd, or at a sporting event. Vocal fatigue can arise quickly from yelling or talking too loudly.

Singers should stay hydrated by drinking plenty of water. Smoking is not healthy for the body or the voice. Avoiding secondhand smoke is also important. Washing hands frequently with soap and hot water is a good way to avoid germs that humans transmit with their hands. Singers should also be wary of contact with people who have colds or infections.

Singers should be aware that some medications may adversely affect the voice. Over-the-counter medications and herbal or "natural" remedies require as much scrutiny as prescription medications. For information on medications, it is best for singers to consult a medical doctor, preferably an otolaryngologist (ear, nose, and throat doctor). A laryngologist is the most specialized voice doctor available.

Certain foods and liquids can affect the voice by causing dryness or generating excess mucus on the vocal folds. Not all foods and liquids affect individuals in the same manner, however, and singers must learn to predict these effects on their own.

In general, good physical, emotional, and mental health is the ideal for singers. What is good for human health is almost always good for singing health.

Notes

1. The word *larynx* should sound like "minks," not "mix."

2. William Vennard, *Singing: The Mechanism and the Technic* (New York: Carl Fischer, 1968), 52–53.

3. All images in chapter one are from Barbara M. Doscher, *The Functional Unity of the Singing Voice*, 2nd ed. (Lanham, MD: The Scarecrow Press, 1994). Used with permission.

4. Richard Miller, *The Structure of Singing: System and Art in Vocal Technique* (New York: Schirmer Books, 1996), 249–251.

5. Miller, *The Structure of Singing*, 30.

6. Miller, *The Structure of Singing*, 25.

7. Miller, *The Structure of Singing*, 23–25.

8. Miller, *The Structure of Singing*, 24.

9. For additional information on the science of resonance, refer to the published works of Johan Sundberg or Ingo Titze; see Bibliography.

10. Manuel Garcia II, *The Art of Singing, Part I* (Boston: Ditson, c. 1855), 6.

11. James McKinney, *The Diagnosis and Correction of Vocal Faults* (Nashville, TN: Genevox Music Group, 1994), 118.

12. Dan H. Marek, *Singing: The First Art* (Lanham, MD: The Scarecrow Press, 2007), 93.

13. Vennard, *Singing*, 191.

CHAPTER TWO

~

Physiological Issues
of the Choral Ensemble

Within the context of the solo singer in the choral setting, several topics relate directly to human physiology. The topics discussed in this chapter have a great bearing on singers, whether in the studio or the choral ensemble, and reflect the diversity and complexity of the choral environment.

Physical Maturation and Age

Most college-age students are just coming out of their adolescent growth spurt, and their laryngeal development is not yet complete.[1] Dr. Ingo Titze explains how development continues during the college years:

> Even beyond the major growth spurt, development continues up to about age twenty. . . . Under normal conditions of health, nutrition, and exercise, the human voice is relatively stable over about four decades (age twenty to sixty).[2]

On average, college students have not completed physical development until at least their junior year; therefore, if the student's larynx is not physically stabilized, vocal technique cannot be firmly established. It is imperative to note that a physically stabilized larynx does not guarantee a consistent and healthy vocal technique. Because the laryngeal cartilages begin to ossify in the third decade of life, the college student possesses a larynx that is, essentially, less developed than the rest of the body. Titze explains:

> It is known that laryngeal cartilages ossify (turn to bone) with increasing age. The process begins in the third decade and is completed in the eighth. We

might speculate that a partially ossified laryngeal framework can better support the tension of the vocal folds because bone tends to deform less than cartilage under the same stress.[3]

Singers need to know the basic anatomical structure of their instruments. Just as a violinist knows the name of each part of the violin and how it functions, singers should know how their vocal mechanism is formed and how it functions. For example, the young solo singer may benefit from the physiologic knowledge that the larynx is not fully formed in the late teens or early twenties.

Singers also need to know that age and physical maturity can influence which genres of choral music they can sing. When singers are younger, for example, their range is more limited and they may not be able to sing the highest or lowest pitches of their voice parts. They may also find that the demands of certain composers are too much for their young voices to sustain for an entire piece. Such demands may include singing at the extremes of the range, vocal lines that move throughout all the registers, and an especially large accompanying instrumental ensemble. The physiologic limitations of the young instrument should be taken into consideration whether the student is in an hour-long rehearsal or a week of many rehearsals.

Physical maturation continues during the collegiate years, and applying the most efficient, least harmful vocal technique will ease these physical transformations for developing young singers.

Issues and Solutions

ISSUE: The average-aged college student does not have a fully formed larynx and laryngeal framework. This may limit how much and to what extreme singers should use their voice in solo or choral singing.

SOLUTION: There is no "solution" to this physiological reality, but singers must be aware of how their physical development corresponds with their vocal development.

ISSUE: Some choral literature is too vocally demanding for the young singer.

SOLUTION: This issue is equally present with regard to solo literature. The range and *tessitura* of the vocal line may be too wide; certain passages may be sung at an extended loud or soft volume; notes at the extreme ends of the range may be sustained; or difficult passages may fall in the *passaggio*. Ultimately it is up to singers to recognize when the vocal line of a choral piece is overwhelming to their voice, and to decide how to handle the situation vocally. Developing singers should err on the side of caution.

Teaching Example

Claire, a soprano, is a 19-year-old freshman in a demanding choral ensemble at a Big Ten university in the Midwest. She is unable to sustain her voice while singing the Soprano I part in major choral works. At the end of most rehearsals she experiences significant vocal fatigue.

Claire came to the program with much choral singing experience, but the ensemble she was placed in performs large choral works with symphony orchestras on a regular basis. The repertoire of this particular ensemble is wide-ranging and challenging to the young singer. She is a light-lyric soprano, with a lovely and small-sized voice, and she is just starting to learn how to navigate her top voice.

In terms of physical development, Claire is still years away from having a fully formed larynx. She is overusing her voice in choir by singing in the most taxing portion of her range most of the time.

The primary concern in Claire's situation is her regular vocal fatigue after choral singing. Even though she is a high soprano and the choral conductor has placed her in the correct part for her voice, Claire is still quite a young singer and does not have a fully developed technique. She would probably be better served by moving to the Soprano II part in the ensemble. She can still participate in the ensemble, but should not utilize the upper extreme of her voice on a regular basis. When she is older, she can move back to Soprano I.

Challenging *Tessituras*

Young singers may possess a limited range, and may fatigue easily when singing in challenging *tessituras* (pitches within a certain range) for extended amounts of time or at a loud volume level. Moreover, they may not be aware of their own limitations. These factors apply in the choral environment *and* in solo study, but the choral environment may present unique dangers. The *tessitura* in choral literature can sometimes encompass a larger range of pitches than the young singer can handle vocally. Because of laryngeal limitations, the young voice sometimes cannot meet the demands of an individual choral melodic line and may fatigue more quickly in a choral environment than in a solo one.

When choosing solo literature for a young voice, the teacher can take the time and initiative to find just the right piece that fits the voice. Choral conductors do not have this option, since they must consider the vocal abilities of an entire group of singers when choosing repertoire. In other words, conductors must choose the same repertoire for singers of differing skill levels, while the voice teacher can choose for one voice.

In one-on-one vocal study, a singer has the option of bringing a song to the teacher and saying, "This does not sit well in my voice" or "I am not able to handle this piece vocally." In the choral ensemble, the individual singer's needs are not the primary consideration, and a student may not feel comfortable speaking to the choral conductor in the same manner. It is especially important, therefore, that choral singers pay close attention to the level of comfort in their assigned voice part. For example, if a woman is assigned to Alto II and has trouble singing in her upper-middle and top voice immediately following a choral rehearsal, this could indicate that that moving in and out of the chest register for an extended amount of time creates excess vocal fatigue. Or, if a man singing the Tenor I part cannot phonate pitches in his upper register (above F4), he thus cannot sustain that vocal line in choral rehearsal and needs to move to a lower part.

Ultimately the choral conductor and the voice teacher both want capable, healthy singers, and they should have a strong mutual interest in finding the best possible vocal part for the solo singer. A responsible choral conductor should be willing to discuss options with singers when it comes to finding the most comfortable voice part. At the same time, the voice teacher has a responsibility to ensure that the voice student is singing the appropriate part in the choral ensemble.

Issue and Examples

ISSUE: The *tessituras* in choral literature can be challenging for the young voice, as in the following examples.

Examples of Challenging *Tessituras*

Soprano Part, "Let All the Angels," G. F. Handel's Messiah

In this piece, Handel has the sopranos returning again and again to notes above the staff. This vocal challenge is demonstrated particularly well in mm. 22–25. While the part is not sustained above the staff, the return to the top notes affects the voice production of the middle voice as well. The climbing vocal line moves through the second *passaggio* to the top voice.

let all the an - - - - - - - - gels of God wor - - - - - -

Handel's *Messiah*, "Let All the Angels" soprano line, mm. 22–25.

Alto Part, "Blessed Are the Men Who Fear Him," Felix Mendelssohn's Elijah

This piece demonstrates the extreme lower range that can be required of altos in choral literature. The G below middle C in m. 48 is not easily accessible to most women in full voice, and they may find it difficult to move upward from a pitch this low.

Mendelssohn's *Elijah*, "Blessed Are the Men Who Fear Him" alto line, mm. 48–49.

Tenor Part, "Lacrimosa," W. A. Mozart's Requiem

This example shows how the tenor is required to sustain a pitch at the top of the second *passaggio* for several measures. This can lead to fatigue quickly if not sung properly. The pitches must be fully supported with the abdominal muscles, the airflow should move freely and without constriction, and the vibrato rate should be even.

Mozart's *Requiem*, "Lacrimosa" tenor line, mm. 10–18.

Bass Part, "And He Shall Purify," G. F. Handel's Messiah

In this example, the bass part lingers in the top middle voice, which may not be the most comfortable range for a true bass. The bass-baritone may need to switch to the Tenor II part if the bass line is out of his comfortable range.

Handel's *Messiah*, "And He Shall Purify" bass line, mm. 15–25.

Teaching Example

Sadira, a soprano, is a first-year graduate student at a conservatory in the Northeast. She is 23 years old and has a medium-sized voice that is most comfortable in the top register. She has sung in choir her entire life and plans to pursue a career in opera or professional choral singing, or both. She knows she will need to find a church job after school when she moves to a large urban setting, and she wants to gain experience singing advanced choral literature.

Sadira sang Soprano II for her college career, and halfway through her first year of graduate school she is still singing Soprano II in chorus. In recent lessons, her teacher has noticed that she can vocalize higher and higher, up to F#6, and can easily sustain notes in that range of her voice. Sadira tells her teacher that her most comfortable top pitch in undergraduate study was a B5, but since the summer her top voice just "feels easier." Sadira is unsure which part is best for her in the choral ensemble.

Sadira is at an age when the voice can experience dramatic change. As she has aged and solidified a technique, her voice has soared upward. A particular challenge in this situation is that Sadira is focusing on very high operatic literature in her voice lessons and practice, and singing mostly in her middle voice in choral rehearsal and performance.

The situation Sadira finds herself in is not insurmountable! She has two options: staying on the Soprano II part, or moving to a different part. Right now she is utilizing different tessituras in solo and choral work, which seems to be creating a balance in her technique. Singing Soprano II in choir gives her time to rest her very top voice. One option for her is to function as a "pivot singer" in the ensemble— that is, to sing mixed parts in the choral repertoire, Soprano I for one piece and Soprano II for another. She can move between Soprano I and II at the discretion of the conductor.

Independence from Instruction in the Choral Environment

In the private voice studio the singer will learn tonal placement, consistent abdominal connection, breath energy and control, register transitions, and many other skills to aid in voice production. In the choral setting these points are not always addressed, and no one is necessarily guiding each individual voice.

This discrepancy is often ignored, but lies at the foundation of the difference between solo and choral singing. This issue is more urgent in the collegiate or academic setting, as opposed to the community choir, because vocal majors are building their vocal technique during these years.

Most members of a collegiate choir will be students, and most of those students will be music vocal majors. If these vocal majors spend an average of 4 hours per week in choral rehearsal, then by the time they graduate they will have spent a minimum of 512 hours singing in choir. If they have a 1-hour voice lesson per week, they will graduate with 128 hours of singing under the instruction of a voice teacher. That is *four* times more singing *without* individual instruction. Of course this ratio is not always exact, but nonetheless many aspects of students' vocal technique will be developed and solidified during the hundreds of hours they spend singing in the choral environment.

Author and teacher of singing Dale Moore emphasizes this discrepancy:

> In many situations a young singer spends five times as much time per week with the conductor of his or her choral group as he does with his or her singing teacher. If the choral conductor has a strong, dynamic personality and very firm ideas, right or wrong, about vocal technique, need one ask who will have the greater influence upon the young singer?[4]

Of course, as Moore points out, if voice teachers and conductors at a given institution have the same basic views on vocal pedagogy, students will most likely benefit:

> If the ideals of the singing teacher and choral conductor are compatible, choral rehearsals can provide excellent reinforcement for what the singing teacher is trying to do. If the ideals, especially in regard to vocal sound, are very different, the resulting problems can be very difficult for everyone involved.[5]

As stated, typical voice majors—that is, those not matriculating at a conservatory—will spend most of their singing time in choir, *not in* voice lessons or individual practice. How singers produce sound in the choral setting is critically important to their vocal growth and vocal success. On top of maintaining a healthy vocal technique, using the voice wisely, and singing the correct voice part, singers need to take choir as a serious endeavor and preparation for their music career.

Even though singers will not have the benefit of *individual* instruction in the choral environment, they can still receive sound vocal pedagogy from the conductor. Many conductors will take the time to share their knowledge of the voice in an effective way with their ensemble during rehearsal. Choral conductors who are particularly attuned to individual voice production may also offer specific pedagogical insights to a singer during a private moment. Although choral conductors are not focused on individual voice production in choral rehearsal and performance, the astute ones will be aware of an individual's vocal production within the ensemble. The wise singer will carefully consider any vocal input from his conductor.

Issues and Solutions

ISSUE: During choral rehearsal there is no supervision of an individual's voice production.

SOLUTION: Students must monitor their own voices! In the choral rehearsal they must ask themselves, "Am I singing on the breath? Am I consistently utilizing my abdominal muscles? Am I navigating register transitions easily? Am I singing in tune? Am I articulating vowels clearly?" If the answer to any of these questions is "no," they should consult their voice teacher for advice. Students spend a great deal of time in the choral ensemble and must remember to protect their health by maintaining the technique used in lessons and individual practice.

Singers should also glean aspects of vocal technique from the conductor if possible. Of course the conductor is leading a *group* of singers, and may not be as forward in offering technical advice as a voice teacher might during an individual student lesson. Yet singers can still learn by observing the conductor's visual, as well as aural, cues. A gesture the conductor uses may physicalize an important vocal concept. Young singers may not realize that many conductors are trained as singers and use scrupulous language concerning the voice in rehearsal.

ISSUE: During the critical developmental years (approximately ages 18 to 21), most students spend more time singing in choral rehearsal than individual practice.

SOLUTION: Participating in a choral ensemble is not the same as practicing as a soloist, so singers should make daily vocalizing part of their regular practice routine. In addition, singers should maintain excellent vocal standards when singing in choral rehearsal, so that their ensemble work *enhances* their solo practice and development.

A singer's awareness of voice production is as critical during choral rehearsal as it is in individual practice. While in choral rehearsal, singers can scan the body for held tensions, adjust the seated and standing positions for better comfort and production, keep the entire body involved in production, and stay mentally connected to the abdominal musculature.

Teaching Example

Joshua, a tenor, is a 19-year-old freshman voice major. He is in a demanding choral ensemble at a large university in the Midwest. He does not have much vocal training and was accepted to the voice program based on his natural talent, not his vocal experience.

In Joshua's private lessons, his teacher—after a few weeks of working on basic concepts—has observed him inhaling at about 30 percent of his capacity and approaching top notes with a great deal of laryngeal tension. Joshua seems very uncomfortable, even stunned by his own top notes and their lack of quality.

When his teacher asks him how his individual practice has been coming along, he replies that the only singing he has been doing is in choir. He also says that his time in the practice room is "boring" and that he doesn't "know how to practice." The teacher realizes that Joshua has been considering choir rehearsal his practice.

The plain truth is that some voice students, freshmen in particular, do not understand or accept the concept of individual practice. In Joshua's case, he thinks choral rehearsal is enough singing outside his lesson. He practices alone just enough to learn the pitches and rhythms of his solo repertoire. Outside the lesson time, he is not focusing on his technique at all. Because he is not assimilating concepts from his voice lessons in practice, his bad habits from high school have worsened in the context of choral rehearsal and performance. The demands of the literature and newness of the environment have only worsened the situation. In addition, Joshua has no concept of how to monitor his own voice in the choral ensemble. This lack of awareness has led to increased laryngeal tension and shallow inhalation. His teacher has let too much time pass before discussing the practice regimen with Joshua. If the teacher had brought it up earlier, he would have quickly learned that Joshua was not practicing outside his lesson. The teacher had attributed Joshua's lack of vocal progress to his freshman status.

In a frank discussion, Joshua and his teacher can plan a specific practice regimen for him to follow each day. Joshua needs a precise practice schedule to aim for—say, thirty minutes a day, five times a week. Joshua also needs advice on how to monitor his voice in the choral ensemble, and how to focus on his own technique while meeting the demands of the literature and conductor.

With some basic concepts and a practice plan, Joshua should be able to increase his awareness, improve his technique, progress more quickly, and sound better!

Singing by Sensation

What is singing by sensation? This phrase is used often by teachers of singing when talking to students about singing in challenging environments. Singing by sensation is the act of utilizing muscle memory, practice habits, and resonant sensations to sustain a healthy technique when auditory feedback is not available. Most younger singers will not yet know how to sing by sensation.

Singers cannot hear themselves in choir as well as they can in the private studio. Moreover, students in chorus will be focused less on voice production and more on sight-reading, count singing (singing rhythmic values rather than text), phrasing, and uniform production of vowels and consonants. These technical demands can be distracting from basic voice production, which makes singing by sensation essential in the choral setting.

Voice teacher Marcia Baldwin explains the significance of singing by sensation:

> It's important to have students *feel* rather than *listen* to themselves. You cannot hear yourself the way you are heard by listeners. Acoustics differ with varying performance space. You can sound one way in your teacher's studio, another way in the practice room, another way at home, another way in a hall like the East-man Theatre, which has 3,300 seats. Everywhere is different. As singers, we're out there all by ourselves. We need to have a frame of reference to know whether we're on target or not, and that is to feel the buzzing going on in the mask area.[6]

Why learn to sing by sensation? At auditions, competitions, and perfor-mances, singers constantly perform in different physical spaces. The acoustics of any space are affected by dampers such as carpeting and drapes, the size and amount of furniture, the number of people present, and many other fac-tors. These factors directly affect the "ring" or liveliness of the space and the amount of feedback the singer receives. In unpredictable situations, singing by sensation is essential to good voice production and health. A common tendency for young singers is to push the voice in unfamiliar situations, and to support with the throat rather than the abdominal muscles. Singers must learn to trust the muscular memory they have learned in practice and at the studio, and to rely on the *feel* of their voice production rather than the *sound* they are hearing in the space.

Issues and Solutions

Issue: Singers who have not learned the concept of singing by sensation in choir may experience additional vocal fatigue.

Solution: Singing by *sensation* rather than by *sound* is critical to vocal health in choral rehearsal and performance. Learning to *feel* the voice rather than *hear* it is the foundation of singing by sensation.

Singers should be able to feel their voices vibrating in their facial mask and pharyngeal spaces. They should also remain aware of the activation of the abdominal muscles when singing. In addition, singers should pay attention to any discomfort in the throat and adjust accordingly throughout the rehearsal.

ISSUE: The solo singer will frequently audition and perform in different spaces where singing by sensation is necessary.

SOLUTION: Because choral ensembles frequently perform in a variety of venues, choral singing is an excellent opportunity for the solo singer to practice singing by sensation. Developing this skill will greatly benefit the solo singer in future solo auditions and performance situations, especially in less than ideal venues.

Vocal Exercises to Improve Singing by Sensation

Resonance Exercise

Singers move up and down by half steps, feeling the resonance when singing "ng" before moving to the [a] vowel:

Hung - a   hung - a   hung - a   hung - a   hung - a   hung - a

Lip Trill Exercise

With the lips loosely, but completely, closed, and the jaw and tongue relaxed, singers move up and down the five-note scale, letting air gently pass over the lips:

(lip trill)_____   (lip trill)_____   (lip trill)_____

Distorted Hearing Exercise

Singers place their hands in front of the ears with palms facing the rear. For additional effect, place folders or musical scores in the same position as the hands. The point of this exercise is to create enough acoustic distortion that the singer must sense, rather than hear, sound. The exercise can be sung in any key that is comfortable:

va_____   va_____   va_____   va_____

Abdominal Connection Exercise
1. Take a deep, low breath.
2. Exhale for eight long beats on a "hissing" (sssss) sound, alternating soft and loud: two beats soft, two beats loud, and so on.
3. When hissing softly, notice the lack of engagement in the abdominal muscles; when hissing loudly, notice the activation of those muscles.
4. *Remember* the sensation associated with the loud hissing—this is abdominal support.

Teaching Example

John, a baritone, is a 21-year-old senior at a prestigious choir college in the Northeast. He has recently moved from the Bass I section to the Tenor II section, after consultation with his voice teacher. The Tenor II classification is appropriate for his voice. He could have been singing this part since his freshman year, but the conductor wanted to utilize his excellent sight-reading skills in the Bass I section. John's ensemble travels frequently and performs in all types of venues, including churches of various kinds, community centers, performance halls, and school auditoriums. After these performances he is experiencing more vocal fatigue than usual, so he has come to his teacher with the question of how he can conserve his voice and still participate in the ensemble.

John is experiencing vocal fatigue because he is unable to monitor his own voice in choral performance. He has not yet conceptualized the practice of singing by sensation. As a result of this, and his recent move to a very different choral part, he is oversinging in a taxing tessitura.

John's teacher needs to talk to him about auditory feedback, as well as the very real effects of varying performing spaces on singing technique. The concept of singing by sensation should be introduced into his lessons and referenced when discussing resonance and sensation. With new awareness of a skill he probably already has but doesn't fully understand how to use, John should experience less vocal fatigue after choral singing.

An important point to keep in mind is that because of the physiological growth process of the human body, especially in the larynx, the voices of singers in their early twenties may not be firmly established within a vocal category. Some voices, especially male ones, may evolve and shift through categories before settling into their most comfortable place.

Postural Issues

A singer's posture is often the first topic addressed in vocal study. One of the most important parts of voice production is the singer's stance, which will influence vocal tone and breath management.

Elizabeth Blades-Zeller outlines the components of good posture:

1. A stance that is buoyant and elastic.
2. The body feels tall and elongated.
3. The body feels centered and solidly rooted.
4. The torso is not slumped nor collapsed.
5. The rib cage feels open and expanded.
6. The body alignment involves the spine, neck, and shoulders, with weight distributed to both feet.
7. The stance has nobility.[7]

The choral setting creates particular postural issues. First and foremost, the singer is holding a folder of music, which may prove uncomfortable if the singer is not used to this posture. The arms may become tense, and the singer can become fatigued. Blood flow in the upper extremities slows down if the arms are held in a fixed position, and spinal alignment may be affected as the head is bent downward to read music.[8] Choral conductors usually suggest "holding the music out in front of you" to better see the conductor. Unless the singer is positioned in the front row, however, the singer's frontal space will be blocked by the heads of other singers. A tightly knit choral formation does not allow room to spread the arms.[9] Solo singers may find this position stifling and uncomfortable if they are used to performing without music in their hands.

Isometric exercises—holding a muscle in a fixed position for a set duration of time, then relaxing the muscle—may be useful for releasing muscular tensions that build up during choral rehearsal and performance. These exercises can be done quietly standing or sitting.

Issues and Solutions

ISSUE: Holding a music folder in a tight group formation can be awkward, and can quickly tire the arms of the singer.

SOLUTION: Singers can take a break during the choral rehearsal to stretch out their arms, increase blood flow, and release tension. They should not allow themselves to keep their arms in the same position for extended periods of time.

SOLUTION: Singers can position themselves on the end of the row, to give themselves more arm room during performances.

SOLUTION: Choral conductors may require that repertoire is memorized, eliminating the problem, as holding music becomes unnecessary.

SOLUTION: Conductors can consider adding space by spreading out the formation of the group. At the same time, singers should realize that the conductor might have a pedagogical reason for a tighter formation.

Exercises to Release Tension While Standing
1. To release stiffness and tension in the legs, execute slow knee bends. Bend knees slightly and hold this position for about fifteen seconds, then stand slowly.
2. To release the shaking in the knees or legs that comes from excess muscular tension during performance, clench all leg muscles tightly (preferably when you are not singing!) and hold for ten seconds, then release all muscles. Repeat several times.
3. To release tension in the arms, change the position of the folder often, as well as the hand position on the folder. Also remember to drop the arms (not the music) at interludes or between pieces.
4. To release tension in the neck and shoulders, squeeze shoulders up and hold for five seconds, release, repeat. Swallow frequently to relax the pharyngeal and laryngeal areas. Turning the head very slightly and slowly from side to side can release the muscles surrounding the larynx. In performance, drop the shoulders whenever they are in a raised position.
5. To release overall tension while standing, raise up on the balls of the feet and hold for several seconds, then resume standing with relaxed knees. Repeat several times.

Teaching Example

Deborah, a mezzo-soprano, is a 45-year-old member of a renowned community chorus in the Northeast. She is constantly frustrated with holding her folder of music. To read the music she must keep the folder a certain distance away from her eyes, but she never has enough room in the choral formation to place her folder out in front of her.

She has tried tilting her body to the side, but feels conspicuous in this position. She has also tried holding her folder down, rather than out, but cannot see the conductor this way. This problem is seriously affecting her enjoyment of the choral experience.

Some conductors prefer a tighter formation than others, and often for legitimate reasons pertaining to the art of ensemble. But Deborah's physical discomfort is negatively affecting her singing, and other singers may be facing the same issue. If Deborah feels comfortable voicing her concerns, the conductor may consider distancing the rows laterally. Deborah can also stand at the end of a row to compensate for extension of her arms.

Singers should also let their opticians know that they read music in a choral ensemble, as they might benefit from special lenses.

Chairs and Posture

During choral rehearsal, how one is seated in a chair is a matter of real concern. As choral conductor Lloyd Pfautsch writes, "It is important that the chairs provide a degree of comfortable support while also encouraging correct body posture for singing."[10] Singing while seated is a necessary skill not only in choral singing but also in opera and musical theater productions.

Since solo singers do not typically take voice lessons from a seated position, they may not realize that sitting can constrict the abdominal musculature and affect the breathing mechanism. Robert Garretson explains how, in his view, the seated position for singing is similar to the standing position:

> When seated, the correct posture from the waist up will be almost identical with the standing posture. The only basic difference is that the legs assume a bent position. While in a sitting position the singer must keep both feet on the floor and lean slightly forward, away from the back of the chair, in order to maintain adequate breath support.[11]

Garretson's viewpoint, however, may run contrary to some basic facts about spinal alignment. If a seated singer, instead of leaning forward, presses the length of his back into the chair, the curvature of the spine becomes less convex, and the head, neck, larynx, and surrounding muscles are in a more free and agile position.[12]

Unfortunately, some chairs used in colleges, universities, churches, and public forums are not designed for choral rehearsal—in fact, some double as desks! In addition, some chairs have a curved back instead of a flat one. Leaning into a curved-back chair can collapse the sternum, crowd the lungs, and impede the breath cycle. Certainly standing is a better option for singers when possible. The combination of long rehearsals, holding music, and inappropriate chairs can bring about fatigue and tension.

One of the biggest hindrances to healthy voice production in the choral rehearsal is the tendency to lock muscles and joints into one position. This can result in reduced blood flow, and possibly dizziness and faintness. Singers should take responsibility for their own comfort. They should also remember the basic tenets of proper singing posture: alignment of the spine; a stretching sensation from the pelvic area straight up through the top of the head; relaxed shoulders; and a raised sternum with plenty of room for the ribs to expand. Awareness of these tenets will allow singers to continually adjust their bodies throughout rehearsal.

Issues and Solutions

ISSUE: Seated rehearsals with improper chairs can present challenges to the solo singer's posture and voice production.

SOLUTION: If the rehearsal is mostly conducted while standing, singers can sit down intermittently and stretch often. If singers are seated for lengths of time, they can remind themselves of the tenets of proper singing posture, and make adjustments.

SOLUTION: Barbara Doscher offers another idea: "Choral singers generally remain stationary during a particular choral work, but between selections and during audience applause they can flex their knees and, perhaps even more importantly, shift their body weight alternately from one foot to another, imitating a slow walking motion. This facilitates the muscle contraction necessary to pump blood back to the heart. . . . Stretching exercises are done with the group as a whole and may include neck stretches, shoulder shrugs, and upward and torso stretches. These exercises, like the stretching exercises used by runners and other athletes prior to strenuous physical activity, will improve blood flow to the upper body."[13]

SOLUTION: Some evidence suggests that a forward-sloping seat helps reduce sitting stress by encouraging the body to mimic the posture of standing upright. Placing some kind of cushion under the sit bones will help achieve this sloping posture, which restores a more natural hip-pelvis-spine relationship and facilitates complete expansion of the rib cage.[14]

Exercises to Release Tension While Seated

1. Elevate the sit bones with a slanted cushion or rolled-up towel.
2. To release tension and fatigue in the legs, place feet flat on the floor, raise toes off the ground, then lower them slowly. Now raise the heels, with the toes remaining on the ground, and lower them slowly. Continue to alternate.
3. To release back tension, press into the back of the seat for one minute, then move forward to the front of the chair for one minute. Continue to alternate positions until more comfortable.
4. When not singing, slowly roll the head and shoulders downward, tucking the chin to the chest and bending the face toward the knees. Hold this position for several seconds, releasing any back tensions, then slowly raise up with the head rising last.
5. To release back tension, set music down, grip left side of chair with both hands, and twist torso toward the left and back again. Do the same on the right side.

6. To release tension from sitting in the same position for a long time, go
to a wall during a break and press the back and head against the wall
with the feet out in front of the body. Bend the knees slowly and move
downward. Hold this position for two minutes.

An Interesting Perspective: The Physiologic Improbability of Choir Arrangements

The array of voice classifications in a choir presents an interesting physiologic issue. Many choral arrangements are modeled on instrumental scores,
but an instrumental ensemble has enough range to cover several octaves,
unlike an ensemble of human singers. Because males and females differ little
in laryngeal size, a choral ensemble cannot cover multiple octaves as adeptly
as an instrumental ensemble. Dr. Ingo Titze speaks of the "physiologic absurdity" of imitating instruments with voices:

> The simple truth is that male-female differences are not large differences.
> Based on the approximate ten percent difference, the linear body dimensions
> simple scaling would give us only a two-semitone difference between average
> male and female voices.[15]

In other words, the extended *tessitura* of choral music is not a simple re-
flection of natural variations in the human voice. Titze further explains why
a choir cannot duplicate the variety of color and range found in an orchestral
ensemble:

> In summary, attempts to cast adult human voices into four-part harmony that
> stretches over several octaves are incompatible with physiologic and acoustic
> scaling principles. Singers and singing teachers need to be aware of this and
> not get too frustrated when vocal ensembles cannot duplicate the range of
> orchestral ensembles.[16]

Titze compares the four-part voices of a choir to a typical string quartet,
but with the cello left out altogether:

> In terms of instruments, the men would be the violas and the women would
> be the violins. It starts with the idea that composers tend to divide things up
> into octaves, generally for good musical reasons and so right away we have this
> dichotomy between bass clef and treble clef, and people don't come that way.
> Naturally, we're not scaled 2:1. . . . The membranous vocal fold, which is the
> most disproportionate, is scaled by 1:6; this is the largest scale factor you can

find anywhere in the body. So at most, females and males ought to be a fifth apart because 1:5 is a musical fifth.[17]

The "absurdity" of voices mimicking instrumental ensembles is less evident in solo singing, as the solo voice presents less basis for comparison with an instrumental group. In any case, it is interesting and important for all of us who participate in choral singing to be aware of these acoustic scaling principles, at least from a theoretical perspective. And theory aside, singers, composers, and audiences alike don't seem to mind the limited scale of the human larynx! Despite the physiologic improbability of choral arrangements, the choral form will continue to be a widely appreciated form of musical expression.

Issues and Solutions

ISSUE: Voice scientists have explained that the extended range of choral singing is a physiologic and acoustic improbability, because of the natural proportions of the human body and vocal folds. Biological differences between the male and female vocal folds would suggest that men and women should sing no more than a fifth apart on average.

SOLUTION: The difference in male and female laryngeal shape and size is a physiological reality, not a problem demanding a solution. A basic understanding of the natural differences between the male and female larynx nonetheless casts an interesting light on the extended ranges found in choral arrangements.

Notes

1. Barbara M. Doscher, *The Functional Unity of the Singing Voice*, 2nd ed (London: The Scarecrow Press, 1994), 241.

2. Ingo Titze, *Principles of Voice Production* (Englewood Cliffs, NJ: Prentice Hall, 1994), 182.

3. Titze, *Principles of Voice Production*, 182.

4. Dale Moore, "A Plea for Dialogue," *The NATS Journal* (January–February 1990): 3.

5. Moore, "A Plea for Dialogue," 3.

6. Qutoed in Elizabeth Blades-Zeller, *A Spectrum of Voices: Prominent American Voice Teachers Discuss the Teaching of Singing* (Lanham, MD: The Scarecrow Press, 2002), 31.

7. Blades-Zeller, *A Spectrum of Voices*, 2.

8. Doscher, *The Functional Unity of the Singing Voice*, 77–78.

9. Doscher, *The Functional Unity of the Singing Voice*, 77–78.

10. Lloyd Pfautsch, "The Choral Conductor and the Rehearsal," in *Choral Conducting Symposium*, ed. Harold A. Decker and Julius Herford (Englewood Cliffs, NJ: Prentice Hall, 1988), 75.

11. Robert Garretson, *Conducting Choral Music* (Upper Saddle River, NJ: Prentice Hall, 1998), 71.

12. Doscher, *The Functional Unity of the Singing Voice*, 79–80.

13. Doscher, *The Functional Unity of the Singing Voice*, 133–35.

14. Brenda Smith and Robert T. Sataloff, *Choral Pedagogy* (San Diego: Singular Publishing Group, 2000), 76.

15. Titze, *Principles of Voice Production*, 186–87.

16. Titze, *Principles of Voice Production*, 187.

17. Titze, *Principles of Voice Production*, 187.

CHAPTER THREE

~

Pedagogical Issues
of the Choral Ensemble

Singers can be assured that many choral conductors care deeply about the health and well-being of the individual voice. Harvey L. Woodruff is one of those conductors:

> I believe that no teacher or musician should be employed as a choral conductor in any school, college, church, or other organization unless he possesses an adequate working knowledge of the instrument he deals with. This means that although he need not be a soloist himself, he should be able to demonstrate methods of voice production both right and wrong and, to a considerable degree, in the classification and guidance of individual voices he should be a vocal diagnostician. I believe that what is best for the individual singer in the matter of tone production is generally of greatest benefit to the chorus.[1]

Choral conductor Edward Byrom agrees:

> The more choral conductors know about the voice, about their own voices, and about the voices of those they conduct, the more effective they will be in achieving a quality choral sound with their ensembles. I have always been an advocate for the individual voice in the choral setting. I feel it enhances the vitality of the choir, lets individual voices sing freely, and allows for a variety of color changes that are necessary for high-level musicality in the ensemble.[2]

Nonetheless, the singer should keep in mind that the pedagogical context of choral ensemble will differ from that of individual voice instruction. As one choral conductor explains, "The ultimate pedagogical contribution every choral conductor should make is to inculcate in all singers the love of singing and of working together on behalf of the choral art."[3]

This chapter begins with a discussion of vocalizing (warming up), as this is the initial activity of singers, whether alone or in a choral environment. The next issues addressed are resonation and individual timbre, both of which are greatly influenced by the choral environment. Respiration is addressed next, followed by intonation, which is of paramount importance to good singing in the solo and choral environments. Finally, modification is discussed, as well as two special categories of choral singers: the nontraditional singer and the amateur singer.

Phonation through Warm-Ups

The primary issues faced by the solo singer in the choral setting include phonation, resonation and timbre, respiration, and registration.

The approach to the vocal warm-up may be very different in solo and choral settings, as the soloist is pursuing an individual goal, while the choir is pursuing the group goal. Soloists choose their own warm-ups according to their individual wants and needs, while the conductor chooses warm-ups based on what he perceives as the needs of the entire ensemble. The purpose of the soloist's warm-up routine is to stretch the laryngeal muscles and prepare the vocal folds to meet whatever demands the *tessitura* and musical style of the literature may require. The soloist uses the warm-up (vocalization) to determine the flexibility, resonance, placement, and quality of the voice on any given day. In other words, singers use warm-ups to cultivate their voices' full color and vibrancy. (For a more complete explanation of phonation in singing, please refer to the overview of voice production in chapter one.)

Warm-up routines vary greatly from day to day and singer to singer. Singers will have a vocalizing regimen that is learned from the voice teacher and used regularly in the studio. When singers practice *vocalises* (exercises), they move from simple to more complex exercises and from the middle of the voice to its outer extremities. Auditory feedback is an important part of the soloist's warm-up. The warm-up may begin with an onset (starting) of the voice, using *staccato* (short and detached) or *tenuto* (held) pitches in the middle voice. The next step may be the cultivation of resonance by humming, singing on "ng," or practicing lip and tongue trills. The singer may then move to agility exercises that move the voice up and down, using the five-note or nine-note scale and incorporating different vowel sounds, including the five basic Italian vowels: [i], [e], [a], [o], and [u]. Next may come a *sostenuto* (sustained) exercise, in which pitches are extended on different vowels and in different registers of the voice. The singer may finish with exercises that extend the range, crossing into all registers and testing the limits of dynamic control. The order and purpose of these exercises have been cultivated over hundreds of years in the Italian *bel canto* (beautiful singing) traditon. Conscientious singers know *why* they are singing *vocalises*: they are the basis of vocal technique.

The warm-up routine of a choir focuses on uniting the group to a common goal.[4] Accuracy of rhythm and intonation take precedence over individual color of tone. Singing the exercise correctly, while "blending" with other members of the choir, is emphasized. Good conductors recognize a dual purpose in their warm-up: to exercise the singers' voices, and to unify the singers in preparation for the ensemble singing in rehearsal.

Sometimes the vocal exercises that a conductor demands at the beginning of rehearsal can be problematic for the solo singer. For example, to tune the ensemble, the conductor may practice chord building in which the basses sing the tonic, the tenors sing the third, and so on. To participate in this exercise, singers have to modify their vibrato rates and adjust their tuning to blend with the rest of the section. Repeated modification during this exercise can slow down the flow of air, fatigue the vocal folds, and disconnect abdominal interaction from the vocal instrument.

A text for choral conductors offers the following statements for the conductor to exhort the ensemble during vocal exercises: for sound placement, "Out of your forehead, not out of your chest!" "Out of your third eye—in between your other two eyes!" or "Out of the chimney on top of your head!"; and for troublesome [i] vowels (pronounced "eee"), "Sing them through your two corner teeth," or "Sing them as though the sound were a screwdriver going up through your hard palate."[5]

Such suggestions are not rooted in voice science or human anatomy, and it is troublesome to see them in a text meant for group voice instruction. Some voice teachers and conductors regularly use such imagery in their teaching with good results. However, a choral conductor communicating with many singers at once should also keep the vocal instruction rooted in voice science. Ideally, voice teachers and choral conductors should gravitate toward the same vocal pedagogy texts.

Precision is the only way the conductor can be certain every member of the group is singing the same thing. Ensemble precision, by its nature, can detract from vocal spontaneity and freedom, which are congruent with balanced laryngeal function. For example, during the warm-up period, solo singers must have the freedom to linger on a pitch while "opening up a note," or to repeat a *presto* (fast) scale if the placement or sensation was not accurate enough. Singers build their voices and solidify their technique by having the freedom to listen to themselves and make needed adjustments. As Ingo Titze suggests, "If the choral warm-up is not tailor-made to you, I would encourage every choral singer to do your own warm-up before going to choir."[6]

Musician Ray Robinson sees no conflicting interests in the choral warm-up:

> It is rather a very special time when the conductor brings the choir together and each singer finds his or her identity in the choral ensemble. It is a wonderful time when the unity and *esprit de corps* begin to emerge in a musical and spiritual environment.[7]

This is a pleasing generality, but in reality the conductor's chosen methods may not mesh with the solo singer's technique! For example, Robinson advises conductors to "combine warm-up exercises with sight-singing sessions."[8] This offers singers the chance to improve their sight-singing skills, but may draw focus away from voice production. Sight-singing is not part of an individual singer's warm-up routine. When singers are focused on sight-reading pitches and rhythms, they may neglect to use their instruments properly. Awareness of these hazards should remedy the situation, and allow singers to vocally multitask. It is imperative that the solo singer remains as self-aware in the choral environment as in private practice.

Again, the goals of the individual and the group must strike a balance. Ingo Titze questions the effectiveness of some choral warm-ups:

> For me, the most bizarre behavior in the rediscovered choir world was group warm-up. Here, the conductor sat down at the piano and played scales or *arpeggios* [chords played one note at a time from lowest to highest]. We all join in, men and women, one octave apart, repeating the exercises in half steps up and down. No mention was made about what the exercise was to accomplish in our voices. Every once in a while the leader yelled out something like "use your diaphragm" or "drop your jaw" or "round your lips."[9]

It is understandable that singers could be confused or frustrated in such situations. Titze continues: "What this type of warm-up totally disregards is the individual nature of human physiology and psychology. Vocal warm-up is a dialogue with your body."[10]

Some may agree that the *individual* nature of a solo singer is what makes a person interesting to watch and hear. Choral conductors may reply that they are working the voice of each individual, so that their goals in warm-ups are not much different than the goals of soloists.

One choral conductor argues that singers should complete their individual warm-ups before choir rehearsal:

> Choral warm-up exercises are not intended solely to warm-up the individual voice, nor should they be. I expect the singers in the choirs here at University of Tulsa to come to the rehearsal "warmed up" vocally in whatever way that speaks to the singer. The choral warm-up is intended to get them thinking and singing together as an ensemble, not as individuals.[11]

A singer's first reaction to this statement could be concern that the conductor is not focusing enough on vocalizing the instrument during the warm-up. On second thought, however, the conductor may be making a valid and important suggestion to the choir, and showing great care for the health of the voice. His suggestion reflects his knowledge that group practice cannot substitute for individual warm-up sessions. Warming up before rehearsal should prepare singers for what lies ahead without risking their vocal health.

Singers who routinely participate in group warm-up without individual warm-up beforehand risk diminishing their individuality and self-awareness. To participate fully in the choral warm-up, the singer must remain acutely aware of himself as well as other singers and the conductor.

Smith and Sataloff offer this general conception of the choral warm-up: "Warm-up procedures are necessary at the beginning of a choral rehearsal to gather the minds and voices of the singers around a common goal."[12] What exactly is this "common goal"? The answer to this question seems to be highly subjective. As choral conductor Howard Swan explains,

> Choral conductors, even more so than teachers of singing, are divided in their opinions concerning vocal technique. Some refuse to employ any means to build voices. Either they consider such procedures to be unimportant, or they are afraid to use an exercise which is related to the singing process. Sometimes the choral director cloaks his own ignorance of the singing mechanism by dealing directly with the interpretive elements in a score and thus avoids any approach to the vocal problems of the individuals in his chorus. Why does a choral conductor attempt to solve vocal problems by avoiding them? Does a singer not need a considerable measure of technical understanding to use his voice properly? It seems sensible to believe that a special quality of teaching and learning are essential for the development of a choral tone which is adequate for the demands of any musical composition.[13]

Solo singers must remain aware that continuous modification of vocal technique in choral rehearsal may have long-term consequences for vocal health. Singers should also realize that some exercises in choral warm-up are designed more for ensemble execution than for individual training. Conductors realize that on any given day, singers may come to their rehearsal having not sung at all, having sung a little bit, or having used their voices a great deal. A reasonable conductor will allow some freedom for the singer in the warm-up portion of rehearsal, especially if he respects the student's work ethic in the ensemble.

Swan's statement illustrates one of the most challenging issues of choral singing: the choral conductor as voice teacher. How can one person possibly attend to the vocal technique needs of a large group of singers? Can the conductor actually teach vocal technique while rehearsing an ensemble? Opera conductors and stage directors do not teach voice in opera rehearsal for a simple reason: they have to direct and conduct the opera!

The choral conductor faces the unique challenge of a group dynamic. In a choral ensemble, there are as many vocal techniques as there are singers. Given these circumstances, perhaps Swan is unfair when he accuses conductors of attempting "to solve vocal problems by avoiding them." An argument can be made that the choral ensemble is not the best environment to teach individual vocal technique.

Issues and Solutions

Issue: In regard to the vocal warm-up, the goals of solo singers and the goals of the choral conductor may not be the same.

Solution: A solo singer can vocalize successfully in choral rehearsal by remaining aware of what each vocal exercise is meant to achieve.

Issue: A group warm-up may not be the best way for a solo singer to vocalize. In the group warm-up, solo singers are not as aurally connected to their voices as they are when singing alone.

Solution: Because of this lessened aural connection, singers may choose to vocalize prior to choral rehearsal. Once in rehearsal, they can participate in the exercises that most benefit their voice production. In some cases, they may even choose not to participate in a particular exercise.

Issue: The vocal warm-up portion of a choral rehearsal is essential to uniting a choir. Singers who choose not to participate in the warm-up process affect the cohesion of the group.

Solution: Conductors have a reasonable expectation that all singers will participate in the warm-up process. The format and execution of the choral warm-up must serve the goals of the entire group and prepare the ensemble to sing specific repertoire as a unit. Solo singers should recognize which exercises are important for group unity and participate in them. Such exercises will help the group improve its intonation, rhythmic accuracy, and vowel unity.

ISSUE: Ensemble precision can detract from vocal spontaneity and freedom, which is congruent with balanced laryngeal function.

SOLUTION: Singers can offset the control and precision required in choral singing with vocal freedom in their individual daily practice.

ISSUE: Some choral conductors may combine the vocal warm-up with sight-singing.

SOLUTION: Singers should not try to sight-sing pitches, rhythms, and text all together when they have not yet vocalized. An individual warm-up before rehearsal may remedy this situation. Also, the singer can sight-sing on a vowel instead of the text to lessen the demands on the voice. Most choral conductors will vocalize the ensemble before moving to sight-singing.

ISSUE: Teaching vocal technique is not the choral conductor's primary purpose in choral rehearsal.

SOLUTION: Singers should apply the vocal technique they learn in individual lessons to choral rehearsal. If they experience vocal problems in choir, they should communicate with their voice teacher. They should also listen carefully to what the choral conductor has to offer in terms of vocal technique, and incorporate those ideas in the rehearsal.

ISSUE: One of the most exciting aspects of solo singing is the individuality and uniqueness of the singer. The choral environment is not conducive to individualism.

SOLUTION: There is great value in solo *and* choral singing. Singers must reconcile themselves to the obvious differences between art forms, and use both experiences to become better musicians and singers.

Teaching Example

Adrienne, a mezzo-soprano, is a 21-year-old junior vocal major at a major university in the Southeast. She sings in a medium-sized women's ensemble and enjoys it very much. The ensemble meets every weekday for fifty minutes, and the conductor always includes a six-to-seven-minute warm-up at the beginning of rehearsal. These choir warm-ups are the only times during the week that Adrienne vocalizes on vowels. She does not include *vocalises* in her own practice because she finds the exercises tedious and does not understand their purpose.

In Adrienne's lessons, her teacher notices that she is singing very differently during the first portion of the lesson (*vocalises*) than the second (*repertoire*). When she is singing repertoire, her voice production has more energy and full body connection. During the vocal exercises, she seems a bit disengaged, distant, and unfocused.

After voicing her concerns to Adrienne, the teacher discovers that Adrienne had stopped including vocal exercises in her daily practice because they were "boring" and she would "rather just get on with the actual singing."

Some students view the process of vocalizing as tedious and irrelevant to their vocal study. In Adrienne's case, her disinclination toward warm-ups as a solo singer has most likely crossed over into the choral rehearsal. Instead of using the warm-up portion of choral rehearsal to focus on her vocal technique, she is thinking of it as something to just "get through." Unfortunately, this lackadaisical attitude has resulted in a voice that sounds very different (and much better) in repertoire than vocalises.

The principal concern in this case is that Adrienne is not relating vocal concepts from the lesson to specific vocal exercises in her individual practice or choral rehearsal. She is unable to sing vocal exercises well, or with her best vocal production. As a result her voice may not be in the best possible shape, and she may have limitations in handling repertoire.

Adrienne's teacher must emphasize that vocal exercises are the centerpiece of a singer's vocal technique. These exercises are critically important for a singer still in physical and vocal development. Adrienne should understand that isolating vowels in vocalises is the best way to optimize coordination and resonance of the instrument.

Her teacher should strongly suggest that she reinstate vowel exercises into her daily practice immediately. They can sit down together and discuss why each vocalise is necessary, so that Adrienne can sing each one with a clear intention. Her teacher should also encourage her to do her own warm-up before and after choir, so she can immediately sense the difference between her choral and solo technique on a daily basis. After implementing this new regime, Adrienne should bring much more vocal commitment and energy to the vocalization portion of her lesson.

Exercises for Individual Warm-up before the Choral Rehearsal

Practice of Onsets

Singers move up and down by half steps:

ma mi ma mi ma   ma mi ma mi ma   ma mi ma mi ma

Agility and Flexibility Practice
 Singers move up and down by half steps, alternating vowels:

Practice of Sustained Phrases
 Singers move up and down by half steps encompassing a fifth:

Practice of Unifying Registers
 Singers move up and down by half steps, as low and high as comfortable:

Individual Warm-up Exercises for Each Voice Type

For Sopranos
 Move up by half steps until as high as comfortable, and then come back down:

For Mezzo-sopranos (Altos)
    Move up by half steps to G Major, then back down:

vi_____ a_____

For Tenor
    Move up and down by half steps:

vɛ_____ i   i_____ɛ

For Basses
    Move down by half steps:

vɔ_____ u_____

Individual Warm-down Exercises for Just after Choral Rehearsal

Slides
    Singers slide down and back up a fifth, singing every pitch in-between:

vi_____ vi_____ vi_____

For Sopranos and Mezzo-sopranos (Altos)
    Singers move downward by half steps as low as is comfortable:

vɛ _____

For Tenors
Singers move up and down by half steps:

va

For Basses
Singers move up and down by half steps:

va

Resonation and Individual Timbre

Ingo Titze defines resonance as "reinforced natural oscillation; literally, a resounding by echoes or other types of enhancement."[14] This "natural oscillation" or resonation has to do with the propagation of sound waves. The individual quality and color of a voice is brought about through phonation and the resonators of the vocal tract. Singers most commonly deal with resonance in relation to tonal placement and tuning of the vocal tract. How and where a singer "places" his voice is integrated into the technique during formal training. The studio teacher should help guide the young singer in the placement of the voice, using location-based imagery when appropriate. Placement must be physically comfortable for the singer, and must assist resonance. A singer's sense of tonal placement may vary according to sex, age, and voice classification.

Smith and Sataloff explain their concept of resonance in the choral setting:

> The singer must learn to trust the sensations of resonance and the admonitions of the conductor. Under the guidance of the conductor, rehearsal—the experience of hearing and feeling—creates a memory of coordinated thought and action and of sounds and sensations for the choral singer.[15]

While singers should trust the sensations of resonance, they must be careful regarding the conductor's admonitions about resonance in a choral setting. Why? The choral conductor is not listening to individual timbres;

he is guiding the group toward a *collective* resonant sound. Johan Sundberg expounds on the issue of voice timbre:

> In any event it seems that voice use in choral and solo singing differs in certain respects that are probably important for the success of a solo singer. It seems fair to assume that students of solo singing who have no problems with their voice timbres could gladly join a choir and, in this way, enrich their musical experience. If, on the other hand, the student has problems in developing an acceptable voice *timbre* and if he or she also has a hard time learning two slightly differing types of voice use at the same time, it seems wiser to concentrate on one thing at a time. In any event, it would be advantageous to know that the same type of voice *timbre* is not sought in choral and solo singing. . . . Choral singers strive to tune their voice *timbre* in order to mesh with the *timbre* of the rest of the choir, while a solo singer would try to develop his or her own individual *timbre*.[16]

In a text written by Frauke Haasemann and James M. Jordon and intended for choral conductors, they make the bold suggestion that the conductor listen to individual students sing vocal exercises in choral rehearsal. The conductor cannot assume that individuals have grasped a particular concept just because the entire group sings it well. They go on to emphasize that this individual singing should not take place until the choir is comfortable with the conductor and the vocalizing process, and the singers have been heard in a private lesson or small group lesson.[17]

Individual performance of vocal exercises is an intriguing idea for choral conductors to consider. While many conductors employ quartet checks (having one singer on each part sing a portion of a choral work), not as many make a practice of listening to their singers vocalizing independently. Conductors could find it very productive to hear students in an isolated vocal context.

Issues and Solutions

Issue: Individual resonance is not necessarily the ideal in the choral ensemble.

Solution: Singers and teachers of singing know that the true beauty of the individual voice and the most exciting aspects of vocal performance are inextricably linked to a singer's resonance. Unavoidably, however, an essential goal of choral performance is to avoid exposure of individual voices. How then do solo singers manage their free, vibrant, resonant timbres during choral rehearsal and performance? One possible solution is for solo singers to sing softly in a half-voice while maintaining their resonance. Another strategy is to lessen the abdominal connection and sing with less overall vibrato and timbre, while keeping the breath moving to prevent the vocal folds from becoming stiff. By utilizing these methods of marking (using less than full voice), singers will produce less sound overall.

SOLUTION: After choral rehearsal, singers can reinstate their sense of resonance by including the following exercises in their warm-down.

Exercises for Increasing Resonance
Recent research by voice scientists has revealed that creating a resistance to airflow where the air leaves the body can have a positive impact on how the vocal folds and vocal tract interact. Humming exercises, when performed correctly and in resonance, help the singer produce sounds that are better balanced in resonance quality.[18]

Humming Exercise
While holding the first pitch, singers flip the bottom lip with the finger. If sound emits, the singer is in resonance; if no sound emits, the singer is in nasality:

Another Humming Exercise
As they sing down the fifth, singers should keep the lips pressed loosely together and feel them buzzing:

Exercise to Increase Resonance
Singers linger on the first note of every pair until they feel a buzzing in the lips; then they move to the open [a] vowel. Repeat with [m] and [n]:

Teaching Example

Rachel, a soprano, is a 17-year-old freshman attending a small liberal arts college in the Midwest. She had a home-schooled education and never participated in a choral ensemble until college. Two months into the new semester, her teacher is noticing nasality in her singing, especially in the upper-middle and top voice.

Rachel's lack of resonance and excess nasality is most likely due to inexperience. Another contributing factor may be that she is singing much more than she ever has, between lessons and choral rehearsal. In all likelihood, the choral ensemble is not the issue here. Rachel just needs to learn how to practice effectively. Specifically, she needs to immediately incorporate resonance-building exercises into her routine. Only Rachel's awareness and determination can turn this problem around, but change is possible!

Respiration

Respiration is essential to vocal technique. In choral and solo singing the essence of breath management is the same, while the *execution* of breath management differs.

A singer performing an aria or *lied*, for example, will execute every sung phrase on one breath, and decide where to place the breath based on the melodic line, text placement, and other vocal issues. An inhalation usually prefaces a new phrase, while in choral singing an individual's renewed breath may or may not indicate a new phrase.

Solo singers may improve their breath capacity with each new piece studied. The student and voice teacher work to coordinate breath as it applies to the musical language and text setting. In slow, sustained passages, for example, students may use a slightly different technique than they would for *coloratura* passages. Most importantly, the student learns to isolate the inspiratory phase from the expiratory phase. Titze explains:

> In the inspiratory phrase, abdominal muscles need to be trained to relax quickly and completely to allow maximum downward movement of the diaphragm. This sudden "collapse" of abdominal effort, with a bulging out of the midsection, may be difficult for two reasons. First, some people almost chronically engage the abdominal muscles as a corset, to tuck in their bellies. Letting go of the midsection may be tantamount (psychologically) to letting one's pants drop. Second, the abdominal muscles are used extensively to provide breath support (adequate subglottal pressure) in the expiratory phase. Vocologists who do not distinguish clearly between the inspiratory and expiratory

phases may have their students or clients keep the abdomen tight all the time. Not only could this waste energy, but also it could restrict air intake.[19]

Smith and Sataloff define choral breathing as "a corporate feeding of the choral tone." They go on to explain that "no one singer will necessarily execute any phrase in one breath."[20] Of course choral singers often do execute phrases in one breath, but they are more likely to take breaths in the midst of a phrase than singers performing solo literature. Solo and choral music are composed with these important differences in mind. A composer conceives an aria for one voice, and this is reflected in the shape and length of vocal phrases. The choral composer, on the other hand, has the luxury of writing for several singers per part and is not limited by what one voice can execute.

When singers of an ensemble inhale at different points in a musical phrase, this is known as "staggered breathing." Singers who engage in staggered breathing in choir may find the practice creeping unconsciously into their solo singing.

If singers can treat choral staggered breathing as they would a series of catch breaths (low, quick inhalations that accommodate the demands of the vocal line) in solo singing, they will have a greater chance of maintaining consistency between the two environments.

Issues and Solutions

ISSUE: Musical phrases in choral literature are not composed for the solo voice and require different breath patterns than solo singing.

SOLUTION: In choir, singers can use the same catch breath that they use in solo literature. For solo singers, choral rehearsal is a great time to monitor their inhalations for a catch breath and make sure they are inaudible.

ISSUE: In choir, many singers do not realize they are making noisy inhalations. Feedback from other singers masks the noise.

SOLUTION: Singers should remind themselves that inhalations are silent. Choral rehearsal is a good time to practice a low, wide, and silent inhalation. Any kind of phonation during the inhalation indicates that the cords are somewhat approximated. Silence during inhalation indicates a fully open glottis.

ISSUE: When practicing staggered breathing in the choral ensemble, singers in the same section will often make their inhalations at the same time, leaving certain pitches unsung.

SOLUTION: This is a common and challenging occurrence in choir. If a section only has a few members, they might mark in the score where each person is supposed to breathe, so that no pitches are left unsung. At the very least, singers can confer with the choir members on their left and right to coordinate staggered breathing.

Exercises to Improve Breath Management

Increasing Breath Capacity
1. Take in a full, low breath, beginning the inhalation with an all-around expansion of the rib cage.
2. Make the inhalation last for five long beats.
3. Hold the expansion for five long beats, feeling the space around the ribs and the low expansion of the rib cage.
4. Exhale for five long beats, letting the rib cage slowly collapse and the recoil extend over the entire five beats.

Connection of Breath to Abdominal Muscles
1. Inhale for four long beats.
2. Exhale over eight long beats while making a strong "hissing" sound (sssss).
3. Maintain awareness of the connection to the abdominal muscles and the constancy of the hissing sound.
4. Repeat.

Quick Inhalation Exercise
1. Take in a quick, low breath.
2. Be sure to release the lower stomach muscles for full expansion.
3. Hold this position for ten seconds.
4. Notice the rib cage expansion in the front and side of your body.
5. Slowly release air.
6. Repeat.

Teaching Example

Daria, a mezzo-soprano, is a 20-year-old vocal major at a liberal arts college on the West Coast. She participates in a medium-sized choral ensemble. She auditioned for and won a solo for the choral concert at the end of the year. Her voice teacher attended the concert and thought she sang beautifully, except for one problem. She was standing about two feet away from a microphone and made a very loud gasping inhalation before singing each phrase. This was very distracting to the teacher and probably to the audience as well.

Audible inhalations are becoming more of a problem as amplification technology becomes more common in performance. Daria's participation in choral ensemble may or may not be responsible for the loud gasping noise she makes prior to inhalation. Some singers do make a louder inhalation in choir because they don't hear themselves in a group atmosphere. Others make a loud inhalation both in choir and in the solo lesson. Because Daria was delivering a public performance, her nervousness may have distressed her breathing.

If Daria is planning future performances, her teacher should suggest that she watch a video recording of her concert. By observing and listening to herself, Daria will gain a new awareness of her inhalations and performance style.

Teaching Example

Jonah, a bass-baritone, is a 19-year-old vocal major attending a midwestern university. He is working on a well-known *oratorio* aria with long phrases. When he presents the aria to his teacher for the first time in a lesson, he is unable to sing through an entire phrase without losing his breath. His teacher knows that Jonah greatly enjoys participating in choir. Jonah is always happy to attend extra choir rehearsals or sectionals, and wants to participate in more than one choir. The teacher also knows that Jonah neglects his private practice time and considers his time in choir his practice. He only sings in the practice room enough to learn his repertoire.

Most likely, Jonah's issue of breath management has nothing to do with his participation in choir. However, if he prefers choral singing over solo singing, and participates in more than one ensemble, he may not practice his solo technique enough or in the proper manner.

His teacher explains that he must vocalize on a regular basis to build muscle memory and then apply the techniques he is learning in the studio. Jonah agrees to practice more as a soloist, and to pay attention to his breath cycle. His teacher also suggests that Jonah pay particular attention to his inhalation, fully expanding his rib cage and maintaining this feeling of expansion throughout the phrase. After practicing deeper inhalations in his practice sessions and choral rehearsal, Jonah should be able to sing the aria with no problem, and his vocal awareness in choir will be heightened.

Intonation

Intonation is equally important in choral and solo singing, but for slightly different reasons. Intonation issues present especially tough challenges for the choral conductor, as vocal pedagogue Barbara Doscher explains: "For the choral conductor, the situation is more complex because of the individualistic nature of each voice and even of the musical background of each singer."[21]

When a *solo* singer sings out of tune, there is no other voice to compare tuning. When a *choral* singer sings out of tune, other choir members provide a reference and tuning problems become more obvious. The technical issues that can cause tuning problems—lowered *velum*, under-energized singing—may not be as obvious in solo singing, as there is no other voice to reference. On the other hand, tuning problems might be obvious even in solo singing.

Choral conductor Paul Roe touches on the myriad causes of incorrect choral intonation:

> . . . the effect of acoustics on pitch, the effect of atmospheric conditions upon pitch, the relationship of correctly produced tones to intonation, physiological factors, the relationship of dynamics to pitch, the relationship of lack of mental alertness to intonation and the inability to hear mentally.[22]

These factors apply to both choirs and solo singers, but the choir environment presents particular challenges. Singers are affected by the singers around them, and may lose control over their intonation. The choral singer hears pitches from all sides, as well as from the piano or instruments. Therefore, it is reasonable to assume that choir members directly influence each other's intonation.

For tuning problems, Barbara Doscher offers solutions such as "Do not sing until you know the music well enough not to tire your voice" and "Sectional rehearsals provide a partial solution."[23] While these are both excellent suggestions for the singer and choral conductor, the fact remains that individual singers cannot completely control their perception of intonation in choir because of the presence of other singers.

Verbal cues from their conductor regarding intonation may be at odds with techniques prescribed by teachers of solo singing. For example, this passage from a choral pedagogical text recommends a variety of dubious intonation instructions:

> When a choral tone is "sharp," some conductors ask the singers to round their lips. Thinking sad thoughts instead of happy, minor moods instead of major may have the same effect. Conversely, if the pitch is "flat," the singers may lift the upper lip slightly, revealing the two front teeth. Putting a sense of joy into the tone of shifting moods from dark to light may help. Sometimes, just asking the choir to smile slightly is sufficient to lift the pitch.[24]

As singers know, "lifting the upper lip slightly" may alter the pitch, but perhaps not in the way desired. At certain pitches, the result could be very unattractive. Using impressionistic words such as "light" and "dark" may work for some individuals, but this approach is not grounded in voice science and should probably be avoided.

Now witness the following statement about intonation from a renowned choral conductor (1965):

> It might be interesting to note that teenaged sopranos are apt to sharp on high tones, while women over forty have a tendency to flat. Youthful enthusiasm accounts for sharping, and flatting might be the result of emotional passivity or perhaps just plain flabbiness.[25]

It is hard to know what offends more: the reference to age, the reference to flabbiness, or the reference to women only. In any case, solo singers can temper suggestions from the conductor with common sense. Singers should use solid vocal technique and the advice of their teacher to correct any intonation issues.

Issues and Solutions

ISSUE: It is almost impossible for singers to correctly interpret their own intonation in choir.

SOLUTION: In regard to choral intonation, a singer's best option is to sing by sensation and trust the vocal technique instead of trying to listen to the voice.

ISSUE: The tuning problems of other choir members affect the choral singer.

SOLUTION: One singer cannot solve the tuning problems of another singer. To help offset the influence of other choir members, singers should do their best to sing in the center of the pitch and maintain as much of their solo technique as possible in the choral setting. For singers with intonation problems in their solo work, it is extremely important for them not to sit next to other singers with tuning problems in the choral rehearsal.

SOLUTION: To ensure good intonation, Barbara Doscher wisely suggests that singers refrain from singing full out until they know the music well enough. If this familiarity cannot be achieved in the choral rehearsal, the singer will have to spend time with the score outside of rehearsal.

Tips for Maintaining Intonation in Choir

1. Always think in the exact middle of the pitch.
2. On held pitches, or when singing an interval upward or downward, make sure there is plenty of vertical space inside the mouth.
3. Trust yourself to sing by sensation when it is not possible to hear yourself.
4. Monitor your throat to make sure there is no feeling of pushing or forcing the voice, as this can cause fatigue and flatting.

Teaching Example

A soprano named Shannon, age 35, is a graduate vocal major at a liberal arts university on the East Coast. She has been singing sharp in her voice lessons. The sharping occurs most often when she approaches a note in her head register from an interval below. The top note of the interval is usually sharp. She clearly hears the sharping on recordings of her lessons and is very frustrated with the situation. On days she is well rested, there is less sharping.

Shannon is a full-time elementary school teacher who takes graduate classes in the late afternoons and evenings. She also has a part-time job as alto section leader at a local church. She is the only trained singer in the ensemble, and the pitch tends to sag low in that section, due to the technique of one or two singers.

Shannon may be unconsciously singing sharply during choral rehearsal and performance in an attempt to raise the overall pitch of the alto section. This could affect her laryngeal muscle memory and become a big problem in her solo work.

It is imperative for singers not to let the technical problems of others affect their singing. However, Shannon is dependent on the income generated by her church job. Shannon could speak to the conductor privately about moving locations in the section, to see if that helps. She can also ask the conductor if he would be willing to work with the singers one-on-one to improve tuning. If there is no other option, she can audition for another church position.

Teaching Example

Julie, a soprano, is an 18-year-old freshman vocal major at a small liberal arts college on the West Coast. She is a very bright student and received an academic scholarship. She auditioned to be a voice major because she loves music and singing. She has not had professional training but possesses a large-sized instrument and has a passion for musical study. The voice faculty recognized her gifts and has high expectations for her.

During her first few weeks of college she noticed that she was vocally tired after choral rehearsal. As she listened to other vocal majors perform in different situations on and around campus, she realized her voice lacked the maturity she heard in others. In her lessons, her teacher noticed that she was not totally flatting but did tend to hover near the bottom of the pitch, especially in the upper *passaggio* (transition).

For the inexperienced singer, the combination of solo study and choral ensemble can be daunting and vocally overwhelming—especially if the student, like Julie, arrives at school without much training.

Julie's flatting problem is probably not caused solely by her choral participation. The main culprits are her lack of vocal experience, insufficient individual practice, and intimidation from other singers. Her teacher should make sure to record their voice lessons so that Julie can clearly hear her tuning problems. Specific vocalises can be applied in Julie's practice time. With the right attention and time to learn, she should start making progress.

Modification

Solo singers who participate in choral ensembles must take particular care not to modify their technique to the point of losing their best sound. Young singers in particular must be very careful to balance choral rehearsal time with individual practice and monitor themselves for balanced laryngeal function at all times.

The teacher of singing should watch out for the most common signs of choral over-modification in the young singer: lessened vibrato or straight tone (no vibrato); shallow or audible inhalation; no self-monitoring of abdominal support; forced placement; nasality or loss of resonance; and general disconnectedness from proper technique and physical production.

Nontraditional Students

In the modern-day academic environment, nontraditional students are becoming more common. Most of these students are older than 21—sometimes much older. An older student is likely to have a more firmly established vocal technique.

Age is very relevant to voice production, and older singers are usually far more technically advanced than their younger colleagues. This difference is an important issue for the young singer, who may try to match the older voice in size, volume, and intensity in choral rehearsal. It is therefore vital that younger students monitor their own voices during and after rehearsal to make sure they are not oversinging.

Despite these age differences, younger students can benefit greatly from the experience and expertise of older students in the vocal academic environment. Many singers return to school in the middle or later stages of their careers to obtain a higher degree for teaching. For the younger student, nontraditional students in choir are a great source of knowledge about the professional world of music.

The nontraditional voice student can be a great benefit to any music program. Young singers should learn from older and more established singers, but not try to emulate their fully developed technique.

Issues and Solutions

Issue: Younger students have a tendency to attempt to match older voices in a group environment. This can lead to oversinging (hyperfunction).

Solution: To minimize the potential for oversinging, younger singers should be positioned next to other singers who are in their age range and do not sing too loudly. They should also monitor their voice production and make adjustments during the rehearsal.

Issue: Young singers may lose solo opportunities in choir to older, more vocally established singers.

Solution: For young singers, the real opportunity is the learning experience of auditioning for a solo. Young singers would be wise to learn and audition for any solo that is appropriate for their voice and skill level. It is a good use of their time to learn the repertoire and practice the art of auditioning. Solid competition from older singers is a benefit to them, even if they do not realize it at the time.

Teaching Example

Darren, a bass, is a 22-year-old junior vocal major at a conservatory with an internationally recognized choral program. He is in several ensembles, and attends many choral rehearsals each week. He has been preparing a junior recital consisting of varied literature.

In his advanced ensemble, Darren is one of the younger members of the bass section. (His school has an excellent graduate program and many of the ensemble students are older.) The conductor of the ensemble changed the singers' positions midway through the semester, and Darren now stands between two older bass-baritones. One is 27 years of age and the other is 34. Darren's voice is secure, but not as large in size, or loud in volume, as the voices of the other two men.

In his voice lesson, his teacher notices that whenever Darren approaches the most intense portion of any song, he tends to get very loud, lose resonance, and become flat quite a bit as a result of oversinging. Darren can hear this clearly when he listens to himself on recordings of his lessons, but the same issue keeps coming up. As his recital date approaches, both he and his teacher are beginning to get nervous. The teacher is especially baffled, since Darren has never had tuning problems in their three-and-a-half years together. He also has a good-sized voice and does not need to push at all!

After talking to Darren, his teacher discovers that Darren has a lot of vocal fatigue after choir rehearsal each day, and lost his voice completely the day after the last choral concert.

Since Darren has not been pushing or pressing his voice when singing alone in previous years, the problem is probably a result of his recent move in choral rehearsal. It seems that Darren has been in the habit of unconsciously emulating the older singers he stands between. Also contributing to the problem are Darren's habit of ignoring proper vocal technique in the choral ensemble; the lack of acoustic feedback; and the acoustic load of the other singers. Darren is responding by oversinging (hyperfunction), resulting in a loss of resonance and tuning problems.

The logical solution would be to move Darren away from the older singers in choir and place him next to singers closer to his own age. Standing on the end of a row in the back could eliminate some of the feedback from other singers and restore Darren's acoustic awareness of his instrument. Darren can be more careful with his technique in choral rehearsal and performance, and resist the urge to always sing loudly in choir. This new awareness, and conservation of the instrument, should eliminate the vocal fatigue and bad habits that Darren's teacher has seen in the vocal lesson.

The Amateur Choral Singer

Untrained amateur singers may come to the choral setting with certain disadvantages. They may not have the necessary skills to make vocal adjustments when the level of music becomes difficult. Amateur singers may not have the stamina to sustain tone throughout long rehearsals. They may not have a wide enough range to accommodate different registers and *tessituras*, and may not have the breath capacity to sustain long phrases. All of these problems result from a lack of training and experience, and can be improved upon with vocal study outside the choral ensemble.

On the other hand, amateur choral singers may have certain advantages over singers with more vocal experience. For instance, amateur singers may be better able to absorb the conductor's advice without "filtering" it through the doctrines of their voice teacher. Amateur singers enjoy choir as their principal singing venue, and can be more willing to try new things vocally without over-concern for their solo technique. They bring an attitude of openness to the choral experience as a whole.

The amateur choral singer may occasionally feel intimidated by other singers in the ensemble. It is important for amateur singers to realize that seemingly more able or gifted singers are not always what they seem, and a more experienced singer is not necessarily the best choir member. If amateur singers feel frustrated with their vocal technique, and this frustration interferes with their enjoyment of the choral experience, they may want to seek out professional training.

Amateur choral singers who want help with specific techniques should find a voice teacher who is experienced in diagnosing vocal issues and solving problems in a practical manner. In other words, amateur singers are more likely to benefit from a technical teacher who uses a pedagogical approach, as opposed to a teacher who focuses on coaching, musical style, and interpretation over technique.

Amateur singers who seek out a voice teacher should explain their situation in advance of the lesson, so that the teacher can set specific goals for the singer and teacher to attain together. These types of lessons need not continue indefinitely, but if the singer really enjoys the experience, the teacher and singer can expand their agenda and include some kind of solo performance as a long-term goal.

Issues and Solutions

Issue: Amateur choral singers may have deficiencies in their technique that affect their choral singing.

Solution: All singers encounter problems in their vocal technique from time to time. Amateur singers who are interested in voice production may enjoy private voice lessons as a supplemental activity to choral participation. Finding the right teacher is critical, and teacher and student should communicate frankly about what is to be accomplished.

Issue: Amateur singers may feel intimidated by other members of the ensemble.

SOLUTION: Amateur singers do not need to make any apology for their vocal skill. Community and church choirs draw singers from all backgrounds. Singers should remember that they are participating in the ensemble for fun, and can benefit from focusing on the essence and beauty of the music rather than the singers around them. This is true for professional singers as well!

Notes

1. Harvey L. Woodruff, "The Choral Conductor," *The NATS Bulletin* 10 (1953): 14.

2. Byrom is quoted in Ingo Titze, "Edward Byrom's Reply to 'Choir Warm-Ups: How Effective Are They?'" *Journal of Singing* 58 (September–October 2001): 57–58.

3. Lloyd Pfautsch, "The Choral Conductor and the Rehearsal," in *Choral Conducting Symposium*, ed. Harold A. Decker and Julius Herford (Englewood Cliffs, NJ: Prentice Hall, 1988), 95.

4. Barbara M. Doscher, *The Functional Unity of the Singing Voice* (London: The Scarecrow Press, 1994), 238.

5. Frauke Haasemann and James M. Jordon, *Group Vocal Technique* (Chapel Hill, NC: Hinshaw Music, 1991), 68.

6. Ingo Titze, personal interview with the author, December 11, 2000.

7. Ray Robinson and Allen Winold, *The Choral Experience: Literature, Materials, and Methods* (Prospect Heights, IL: Waveland Press, 1976), 157.

8. Robinson and Winold, *The Choral Experience*, 159.

9. Ingo Titze, "Choir Warm-Ups: How Effective Are They?" *The NATS Journal* 56 (2000): 31–32.

10. Titze, "Choir Warm-Ups," 31–32.

11. Edward Byrom quoted in Ingo Titze, "Edward Byrom's Reply," 57–58.

12. Brenda Smith and Robert T. Sataloff, *Choral Pedagogy* (San Diego: Singular Publishing Group, 2000), 109.

13. Howard Swan, "The Development of a Choral Instrument," in *Choral Conducting Symposium*, ed. Harold A. Decker and Julius Herford (Englewood Cliffs, NJ: Prentice Hall, 1988), 25.

14. Ingo Titze, *Principles of Voice Production* (Englewood Cliffs, NJ: Prentice Hall, 1994), 335.

15. Smith and Sataloff, *Choral Pedagogy*, 105–6.

16. Johan Sundberg, *The Science of the Singing Voice* (Dekalb: Northern Illinois University Press, 1987), 143.

17. Haasemann and Jordon, *Group Vocal Technique*, 32.

18. Margaret Baroody, personal interview with the author, June 9, 2009.

19. Titze, *Principles of Voice Production*, 75.

20. Smith and Sataloff, *Choral Pedagogy*, 154.

21. Barbara Doscher, "Exploring the Whys of Intonation Problems," *Choral Journal* 30 (1991): 25.

22. Paul F. Roe, *Choral Music Education* (Prospect Heights, IL: Waveland Press, 1983), 102–11.

23. Doscher, "Exploring the Whys," 25.

24. Smith and Sataloff, *Choral Pedagogy*, 167.

25. Olaf C. Christiansen, "Solo and Ensemble Singing," *The NATS Bulletin* (February 1965): 17.

CHAPTER FOUR

~

Pedagogical Issues of Vibrato

The individual rate or speed of vibrato is an important issue for the developing solo singer in the choral setting.[1] While participating in choral music, the singer will have to adjust the vibrato rate (modification) to suit musical styles, the other singers, and the intent of the conductor. Adjusting the vibrato rate may not be a simple matter for some singers. A universal trait of classical solo singing is a pitch-centered but vibrant and free sound. This vibrancy is accomplished by a combination of relaxed laryngeal musculature and free-flowing air.

William Vennard explains the essence of vibrato: "If a tone is well produced it will have the fluctuation I have described, five to seven times per second, with a variation in pitch, intensity and timbre."[2] Vennard goes on to explain how vibrato has created difficulties for choral conductors:

> Choir directors began listening to the two pitches of the vibrato, neither of which is the desired one. Furthermore, in an ensemble, one singer's vibrato was going up while another's was going down, and there are different rates of vibrato. So the theory developed that perfect intonation was impossible except with a straight tone.[3]

In the formative years of college, singers should cultivate a stable vibrato rate, which often indicates a healthy technique in a trained voice. If a choir conductor insists on no vibrato the majority of the time, singers may find their technique challenged.

Ingo Titze explains how vibrancy indicates health in the voice:

> If the vibrato has not been established, it is a sign that the muscles aren't freed up and they are still fighting each other a bit. They are not playing against each other and undulating.[4]

The director of choral activities at Oberlin College Conservatory of Music, Hugh Ferguson Floyd, is sensitive to the needs of the young singer in choir:

> In voice studios with freshmen and sophomore students, the teacher is trying to get a consistent vibrato rate and I want to do everything I can to assist them in the studio. . . . I use straight tone as seldom as possible.[5]

Floyd advocates open communication between choral conductors and voice faculty about individual students and studio teaching concepts. He also recommends that choral conductors use vocabulary similar to that used by the voice teachers at Oberlin: "I use language that matches what they are hearing in the studio."[6] Changing attitudes and open lines of communication are needed so that the choral conductor and voice teacher can cooperate with students' vocal development.

In an attempt to move away from a non-vibrato sound, choral conductor Olaf Christensen called his preferred vibrato "stabilized vibrato." As William Vennard writes,

> Today [choirs] are moving gradually away from the ideal of no *vibrato*. The internationally celebrated St. Olaf Choir once gave impetus to the use of the straight tone, but Olaf Christensen prefers a "stabilized *vibrato*" in which "the pitch deviation is limited to a reasonable extent."[7]

Richard Miller isolated national schools of thought concerning vibrato. For example, the German rate of vibrato tends to be slow, the Italian and English schools medium, and the French school fast.[8]

Research that evaluates the vibrato rates of choral and solo singers is presently in development. Forthcoming scientific studies will soon offer concrete data, for the first time, demonstrating the effects of the choral environment on an individual's vibrato rate.

Many choral conductors agree that prohibiting vibrato runs contrary to the very nature of the human voice:

> To stifle the natural *vibrato* of the human instrument in group performance makes as much sense as expecting the flutes or strings of a fine symphony or-

chestra to play with straight tone. I am convinced that insistence upon it is one of the greatest deterrents ever devised to vocal freedom and the development of the individual voice.[9]

In the ideal choral environment for the developing or established soloist, the choral conductor will embrace a tonal quality with vibrato. As Floyd states, "When a choir sings in tune with vibrato, it is so thrilling. The overtone series kicks in."[10]

Issues and Solutions

ISSUE: Singers must modify their vibrato rates in the choral environment.

SOLUTION: The solo singer may want to avoid situations where non-vibrato singing is used exclusively, and find an ensemble of an appropriate size that accommodates singers with vibrant tone. Remember that some choral conductors are friendlier toward vibrato than others! There may be a choice of which conductor to work with in an academic setting.

SOLUTION: The solo singer may want to avoid singing the higher-pitched voice parts (Soprano I, Tenor I), where the vibrato rate may be more noticeable to the conductor and listener. Singing mainly in the middle *tessitura* may be the best choice.

SOLUTION: Practicing without modification of the vibrato rate is the best way for developing singers to maintain a healthy vibrato rate and establish the correct muscle memory needed for solo performance. Since modification is necessary in the choral environment, it is critical that developing singers spend more time singing in the practice room than in choral rehearsal.

ISSUE: In choir, an individual singer's technique may be affected by consistent modification of vibrato, as well as the feedback of other singers' vibrato rates.

SOLUTION: The singer and voice teacher must consistently be aware of whether the singer is producing an even and free vibrato rate in solo singing. For some young singers, vibrato modification results in under-energized singing. A reminder to "use the whole body" or to "use more breath energy" could help singers self-correct underutilized vibrato.

ISSUE: Developing singers hear different standards pertaining to vibrato in the choral and studio environments, causing confusion.

SOLUTION: Voice teachers and choral conductors need to communicate about the issue of vibrato in the developing singer. If both parties can use similar language in the studio and choral rehearsal, students will be less confused. Choral conductor Hugh F. Floyd and rest of the faculty at Oberlin

College Conservatory are exemplary in this regard. Floyd cares about the vocal health of his choral singers and makes an effort to communicate with the voice faculty and apply the same vocal terms used in the studio to the choral rehearsal. To generate vibrato, for example, "Increase the vibrancy in the sound" is much better than "Bigger, louder!"

Exercises to Check the Singer's Vibrato Rate and Flexibility

For Sopranos and Mezzo-sopranos (Altos)

Sing the entire exercise, moving faster through the pattern until reaching the final pitch with the fermata. Does the vibrato rate feel even and comfortable? Does the voice move easily through this exercise?

For Tenors

Sing the entire exercise, moving faster through the pattern until reaching the final pitch with the fermata. Does the vibrato rate feel even and comfortable? Does the voice move easily through this exercise?

For Basses

Sing the entire exercise, moving faster through the pattern until reaching the final pitch with the fermata. Does the vibrato rate feel even and comfortable? Does the voice move easily through this exercise?

ve _____

This *messa di voce* exercise will help singers assess their vibrato rates as they move from soft to loud and back to soft. Hold the vowel over eight long beats. If the voice cannot start softly, or *diminuendo* to soft, then it is most likely fatigued. A singer's dynamic control is a sign of vocal wellness.

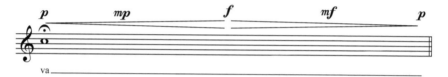

va _____

Teaching Example

Alexa, a soprano, is a 22-year-old senior attending a liberal arts college in the Midwest with a world-famous choir. In addition to her solo repertoire, she sings in an elite ensemble with just a few singers on each voice part. She always sings the Soprano I part when sopranos split, and usually takes the very top notes of a piece. She complains to her teacher that she is struggling with fatigue constantly. She also reveals that the repertoire in choir is particularly challenging this semester, and in two pieces she has to sing quiet, sustained E5, F5, and F♯5 pitches for several minutes. She tells her teacher that while holding these pitches she becomes lightheaded and struggles to keep her tone quiet, stable, and free of vibrato at the same time.

Singing softly is one of the most difficult aspects of vocal technique. The tessitura in which Alexa is feeling the most uncomfortable is the secondo passaggio *area. It is particularly difficult for sopranos to employ* messa di voce *in this range.*

Singing quietly in an ensemble requires some modification of the vibrato rate and slowing down the airflow, which could account for Alexa's lightheadedness. This is a tricky situation for any singer. One of her options is to not sing every phrase in the most difficult parts of a piece. Instead she could alternate, singing one phrase and resting during the next. She could also move to a lower part.

Adult Choral Singers and Vibrato

While this text focuses primarily on the developing solo singer, special mention should be made of the needs and issues of more vocally established singers. Some colleges and universities require their graduate voice students to participate in choir. Graduate students can be almost any age over 21, and this wide age range presents particular challenges for all the singers and the conductor. We have already established that each decade of life brings about further ossification of the laryngeal structure. A singer's individual vibrato rate can be greatly affected by this ossification. Throughout a singer's life, the vibrato quality must be analyzed in vocal study. Adjustments may need to be made in order to increase comfort, and also to eliminate or improve a wider or slower rate. Any vibrato issue a singer has will manifest itself in the choral environment.

Adult singers should be cautious of the demands imposed in the academic environment. They may not be used to the schedule of classes and rehearsals that are typically scheduled during the morning and early afternoon hours. Fatigue is a real threat, especially if they are not used to participating in a choral ensemble. Any variation in the vibrato rate, such as a wobble, should be dealt with immediately so that improper habits do not form. If adult singers practice caution, most will make the adjustment to a new schedule and the rehearsal demands of an ensemble.

Within the choral structure, the conductor must determine how to line up the various vibrato rates of older and younger singers, and individual singers must find a way not to over-modify their vibrato rate, so as to maintain vocal health.

Issues and Solutions

Issue: The mix of young singers with more established singers in the choral environment can result in vocal confusion for the younger singer.

Solution: It is young singers' responsibility to gain awareness of any effect of established singers on their own technique. Young singers should probably stand next to, in front of, or behind singers their own age, so they are not vocally competing with older singers.

Solution: Choral conductors can pay close attention to how they make choral formations with singers of different ages.

Teaching Example

Victoria, a soprano, is a 44-year-old graduate student at a university in the Southwest. She is a professional singer who recently returned to school to earn her doctoral degree. She has spent the last fifteen years working as a singer in Germany and other European countries. As a requirement for the degree, she must participate in one of the school's ensembles. The conductor has many concerns since hearing Victoria at choral auditions. She has a large-sized instrument and a distinctive wide vibrato rate (wobble) that tends to flatten frequently. The conductor has suggested she try the Alto I section, but Victoria will not accept that and insists that she sing in the Soprano I section.

From the very beginning of the semester, Victoria has not fit in with her section. She is much louder than the other women, and her wobble is affecting all of their intonation. The conductor can see that the focus of the rehearsal is the "drama" in the soprano section, not the literature at hand.

This type of sensitive situation can present itself in choral ensembles, especially at large music schools that attract many singers of all ages and experience levels. Victoria's voice, while ideal for Wagnerian operatic literature in opera houses, is simply overpowering in a collegiate ensemble. She is unable to adjust her technique, as her volume level is inextricably tied to her vibrato rate. Her technique has worked well for her over many years of a successful career, so she is reluctant to change it—for good reason.

It is probably only a matter of time before Victoria's choral conductor consults her teacher about the situation. One realistic option is for Victoria to fulfill her choral requirements by serving as a diction consultant for the school's choral ensembles. She enjoys working with languages, and because of her longtime European career, she is fluent in Italian, German, and French. Faculty should consider this type of issue at the initial audition, before graduate students begin their academic work. Places should be made in the choral ensemble for a diverse population of graduate students, but their unique gifts should be properly utilized by the faculty.

The Aging Singer and Vibrato

In religious, community, and even academic choral environments, the aging singer is a mainstay. These singers often serve in group leadership positions or as members of the board of directors. They may also be involved in fundraising and volunteer efforts. They bring maturity and musical experience to the choral environment. At the same time, the aging singer may have particular issues with vibrato. The aging voice can experience alterations in quality and range, including the development of a wobble.[11]

As the laryngeal structure ossifies (hardens to bone), the inner and external laryngeal musculature stiffens and loses some flexibility. The physiological aging process also greatly affects the vocal folds and surrounding structures.

In the past, many have thought that adverse changes to the voice were an inevitable part of growing older. However, recent studies have demonstrated that the effects of aging on the voice are highly variable across the older population.[12] As a *Journal of Singing* article explains:

> Although some age-related alterations cannot be avoided in specific individuals, not all of them are manifestations of irreversible deterioration. In fact, as our understanding of the aging process improves, it is becoming more and more apparent that many of these changes can be forestalled or even corrected.[13]

There is yet more good news for mature singers: research has proven that not all voices change at the same rate, and that physical condition and health have a huge effect on the voice.[14]

Research has also demonstrated that adults who have had vocal training generally sustain their voice function longer than their peers without training.[15] Older singers who are physically healthy and vocalize on a regular basis may be able to enjoy using their instruments much longer than previously thought.

If a singer develops a wobble, it is not astute to immediately attribute it to aging and assume it cannot be improved:

> When we hear a sixty-year-old tenor develop a wobble, we write it off as getting old and are reluctant or embarrassed to challenge him, because, after all, he cannot help aging. . . . However, this reticence is unfair and unproductive. . . . Regular vocal technical training can eliminate the wobble and improve agility, accuracy, and endurance in the older singer as it can in the beginner.[16]

Intelligent choral singers, like great divas of the opera stage, know when they can no longer navigate the voice successfully, and when they must take an exit from the performance environment. Before retiring, however, singers along with their voice teachers and conductors should first take care to examine the situation closely and see if improvements can be made. Vocal study and regular use of the singing voice will prolong the singer's vocal output and longevity.

Issues and Solutions

Issue: Aging singers may have particular issues with vibrato rate, such as a widening or lessening rate.

Solution: With attention and regular practice, most vibrato issues of aging singers can improve greatly.

Issue: For aging singers, ossifying laryngeal structures and other physiological changes may affect their general and vocal health.

SOLUTION: Aging singers who maintain general health and keep their voices in shape can keep singing despite laryngeal ossification. (Interestingly, in the world of professional singing, *female* singers usually retire before their *male* colleagues, and many men maintain a healthy instrument into their seventies; however, this does not hold for all singers.)

Teaching Example

Grace is a 68-year-old soprano who sings in a prestigious community choir with a busy performance schedule. She has participated in the choir for over twenty years and also does quite a bit of fundraising for the organization as a member of the board of directors. Grace used to practice her choral repertoire at home on a regular basis, but in recent months she has been busy and has neglected those practice sessions. At a sectional rehearsal, the conductor notices that Grace is struggling with pitches and rhythms. Of even more concern, her vibrato rate is very slow and can be clearly heard over the rest of the section.

Grace's widening vibrato rate is most likely the result of her lack of practice. Like any other muscles, the vocal folds lose elasticity and flexibility when not used regularly. Some, but not all, older singers may experience stiffening joints and ossification of the cartilages of the larynx. Such factors, along with Grace's neglect of practice, are probably causing her vibrato rate to widen to a wobble.

Daily practice and targeted exercises may help to increase Grace's flexibility and improve her overall tone quality. Also, spending extra time on her choral literature during the week will improve her confidence at rehearsal and put her in a position for success.

Teachers of singing should resist the impulse to recommend that singers drop out of choir because they are "too old." A singer willing to work hard can make positive changes.

Non-vibrato Singing in the Choir

Non-vibrato singing is most commonly referred to as "straight tone." The use of straight tone in ensemble singing is a controversial topic among music professionals. In fact, straight tone use in the choral ensemble is probably the most contentious issue of choral singing for voice teachers. A voice teacher describes the controversy in this way:

> Within today's choral community the questionable concept of non-vibrant and sterile choral sound still has numerous fervent adherents. This philosophy

is handed down through workshops and symposia from one choral conductor to another, permeating North American secondary and collegiate choral scenes. It has taken on the nature of cultism. This search for compliance with a preconceived notion is largely responsible for the turning off of serious singers who should be happily participating in what can be the exciting world of ensemble singing.[17]

Some choral conductors have justified the use of straight tone in choir by invoking historical tradition, from the music of the Renaissance and Baroque eras into the twentieth century. For early music, their contention is that modern-day women's parts were originally written for choirs of young boys, for whom the straight-tone effect was preferred and necessary. Another historical justification for straight tone is that the original music was performed in halls and cathedrals whose cavernous design demanded a non-vibrato pitch for acoustical purposes.[18] In the recent past, non-vibrato singing has still been employed by conductors in well-known choral programs like those of St. Olaf and Concordia Colleges.

Defenders of straight tone thus contend that a modern four-part chorus singing with a straight tone or lessened vibrato best serves the intentions of the composer. Choral conductors also often feel that accurate tuning is more easily achieved with a straight tone rather than a fluctuating one. Ironically, the desired straight tone can often sound out of tune, as vocal pedagogue Barbara Doscher states:

It is better to have a slightly breathy tone with an even *vibrato* and good focus rather than a crystal clear, strident sound with no fluidity. The latter tone often sounds slightly under pitch because the air is being pushed through the resonance tract.[19]

A strident tone can fatigue the voice, and voice fatigue can cause the pitch to drop in concordance. Because the strident tone lacks vibrancy, the laryngeal muscles may contract abnormally, resulting in pitch that can sound flat or sharp.

Pedagogically, non-vibrato singing in choir is a significant issue for voice teachers working with college-age solo singers. Barbara Doscher explains the physical repercussions of straight-tone singing:

The most common kind of over-support puts excessive air pressure on the vocal folds. Such a situation is especially dangerous for young singers because the interarytenoid muscles (adductors of the vocal folds) are still developing and because the extrinsic or strap muscles, which play such a crucial role in positioning the larynx properly, also are still immature. The pharynx is small compared with that of a mature singer, and no amount of wishing or special vocalizing will enlarge it before those extrinsic muscles of the larynx are fully developed (average age of twenty-one or twenty-two), but sometimes later.[20]

For college-age singers, the laryngeal musculature is still maturing and the vibrato is not fully established. Thus choral conductors may be overtaxing their voices by expecting them to conform to a more mature sound. A respected voice teacher *and* choral conductor writes:

It is virtually impossible for a large soprano voice, whose technique is not settled, to supply the vibratoless hoot sometimes desired without greatly retarding her growth as a solo singer, if not causing real damage to her instrument. (Let me stress that in this particular matter I am most concerned for the larger voice.)[21]

As Doscher explains, a young voice that employs straight tone too often in college choir may lose its "bloom":

Generally, the extent of the *vibrato* also must be reduced from that used in solo singing. That singer then may be singing at half-voice, not a condition conducive to functional freedom if continued for any length of time. If the color is altered as well, the voice may never regain its former "bloom."[22]

Professional singer Donald Hoiness expresses his views in plainer words:

Vibrato management is ridiculous and pernicious, when one is dealing with young, unbuilt voices. The urge to control something before it is ready for control is one of my sore points. Students who come up the choral route know control before they know vocal freedom, and in most cases I suspect they never do experience the freely produced, freely supported tone.[23]

When asked if there is a healthy way to sing straight tone, University of Iowa voice instructor and former professional choral singer Susan Sondrol Jones responded:

There is not a healthy way to sing straight tone in relationship to our current understanding of what the classical technique is. As long as singers are trained individually in that school of thought, to place them in an ensemble and tell them to do away with all that individual resonance, color, vibrancy, and control of the breath—with all of the classical training they have had—this will not feel natural. It has to do with muscle memory. . . . In solo singing we work for a vibrant sound, only using a straight tone in instances of ornamentation, to express a mood in the text or for specific coloring change rather than as a tool for the overall sound.[24]

This muscle memory Jones speaks of can be difficult to control in both choral and solo singing concurrently. Just as individual and group musical goals can never be entirely reconciled, the vibrato modification issue reflects an inescapable difference between the genres. William Vennard reinforces this:

> While there is general agreement that *vibrato* is essential to a solo voice, there is a strong group of authorities in the choral field who do not want it in their choirs. Undoubtedly a singer with noticeable *tremolo* (excessive vibrato) can ruin the ensemble, but the cure for this is either to correct the single voice or remove it from the choir. To me, "straight tone" can only be acquired at the expense of quality and I like ringing voices.[25]

A conductor might employ straight tone for a number of reasons: to avoid wobble or *tremolo*; to determine pitch more accurately; to gain rhythmic accuracy; or to establish an overall uniform sound within the choir. A singer, meanwhile, has many scientific and pedagogical reasons to avoid straight tone: undue stress on the vocal mechanism; insufficient air flow and breath support; undoing of muscle memory; spreading of the tone; pitch inaccuracy; loss of overtones; loss of "ring" in the voice; and loss of individual tonal quality.

Richard Miller also sees potential harm in singing straight tone, and offers an unusual suggestion:

> An even *vibrato*, the result of relaxant laryngeal function, is an inherent characteristic of freely produced vocal sound. Choral singers should not be requested to remove vibrancy from their voices in the hope of blending them with non-vibrant voices. Rather, the conductor should assist the *non-vibrato* amateur, through onset and agility exercises, to induce the natural vibrancy of the coordinated singing instrument. Properly produced vibrant voices can be balanced even more readily than can nonvibrant voices.[26]

Miller is contending that advanced singers need not modify their technique as much as the less developed singers need to improve their abilities. While this approach seems logical in theory, most would agree it is not realistic in the academic choral context. In choral rehearsals, the conductor simply does not have time to train the individual voices of less developed singers. Therefore, the conductor's only option is to ask the more advanced singers to modify their voices, or to continue working with the given abilities of the group.

Some experts support the idea that straight tone can be healthy, or even good for training. As Ingo Titze states, "It may actually be a good exercise to learn how to disengage your vibrato, [with] the extent in the singers control."[27] Titze qualifies this by emphasizing that straight tone *in itself* does not signal whether a technique is healthy or unhealthy:

> Vibrato is an indication of good muscle balance, and vibrato-free voice might mean that the person has good balance but disengaged it somehow. But it could also mean that they are totally out of balance with their muscles.[28]

What is the solution for a singer trying to avoid straight-tone singing in the collegiate choral setting?

Conductor Hugh Ferguson Floyd states that "straight-tone singing is tiring" and encourages students "to talk to me and not feel stuck."[29] Open communication between singer and conductor is essential. Floyd also advocates simply dropping out if a specific passage if it is a strain: "In the private studio they can't let go of any note; in choir they can drop out."[30]

Conductor Timothy Stalter facilitates communication on the issue of straight tone through his choice of vocabulary:

> I try not to use the term "straight tone" because straight implies rigidity. When I think "straight," I think straightjacket, I think straightedge, and so I would rather say little or no *vibrato*. [Straight tone] can be fatiguing. You cannot try to make boys out of women.[31]

Conductors should create open lines of communication so that all choral singers are using healthy voice production. Students should seek out an appropriate choral situation that helps them develop vocally and avoid undue strain or fatigue.

Issues and Solutions

ISSUE: Non-vibrato singing is sometimes the preferred tonal quality of choral conductors in certain genres of repertoire.

SOLUTION: The solo singer should seek out a choral situation where straight-tone singing is not employed most of the time. (A group that focuses on music of the nineteenth and early twentieth centuries may be preferable to a group specializing in early music or music of the late twentieth century.)

ISSUE: Non-vibrato singing can fatigue the voice.

SOLUTION: Singers could lessen fatigue by moving to a lower choral part.

ISSUE: Singing regularly with non-vibrato can result in incorrect muscle memory.

SOLUTION: Singers can consciously break off from a non-vibrato tone at certain points in rehearsal. Vibrato is less audible in certain *tessituras*, such as the lower or middle-low voice, so non-vibrato can be reserved for the top voice only.

ISSUE: Non-vibrato singing is at odds with what is taught and internalized in the voice studio.

SOLUTION: Choral conductors need to understand that vibrato is ultimately the more healthy option for singers. If vibrato is not tolerated in the ensemble, the singer can balance time spent in choir with individual practice. After choral rehearsals, singers should warm-down the voice and get the breath and vibrato rate moving as soon as possible. The best choice for singers may be finding a choral situation where vibrato, color, and vibrancy are welcomed.

Exercises to Cultivate Vibrato

Slides to Cultivate Vibrato, for Soprano
Singers alternate closed vowels such as [i], [u], and [o] and slide up and down the fifth, extending the slide as long as possible:

Slides to Cultivate Vibrato, for Mezzo-soprano (Alto)
Singers alternate closed vowels and slide up and down the fifth, extending the slide as long as possible:

Slides to Cultivate Vibrato, for Tenor
Singers alternate closed vowels and slide up and down the fifth, extending the slide as long as possible:

Slides to Cultivate Vibrato, for Basses

Singers alternate closed vowels and slide down and up the fifth, extending the slide as long as possible. Baritones should find the range that is comfortable for their voice:

Ghost Slides to Cultivate Vibrato, Soprano

Use the previous exercise, but instead of a slide, sing with a sliding *motion* while making a ghost sound or shaky vibrato. Make a greatly exaggerated vibrato (as if you are trying to scare someone), but keep it light. Use any vowel, though [u] or even [hu] may be easiest to begin with:

Ghost Slides to Cultivate Vibrato, Mezzo-soprano (Alto)

Use the previous exercise, but instead of a slide, sing with a sliding *motion* while making a ghost sound or shaky vibrato. Make a greatly exaggerated vibrato, but keep it light. Use any vowel, though [u] or even [hu] may be easiest to begin with:

Ghost Slides to Cultivate Vibrato, Tenor

Use the previous exercise, but instead of a slide, sing with a sliding *motion* while making a ghost sound or shaky vibrato. Make a greatly exaggerated vibrato, but keep it light. Use any vowel, though [u] or even [hu] may be easiest to begin with:

Ghost Slides to Cultivate Vibrato, Bass

Use the previous exercise, but instead of a slide, sing with a sliding *motion* while making a ghost sound or shaky vibrato. Make a greatly exaggerated vibrato, but keep it light. Use any vowel, though [u] or even [hu] may be easiest to begin with:

Owl Exercise to Cultivate Vibrato

Singers should approach this exercise with ease. Do not continue to the descending five-note scale until the voice is free of tension. On the final pitch, indicated with a *fermata*, invite vibrato into the tone:

Exercise to Disengage Vibrato

Sing as written, without vibrato, on the open "o" vowel and repeat:

Another Exercise to Disengage Vibrato

Sing a slide up and down the fifth on the [i] vowel, gradually straightening out the tone. Sing the open "e" vowel with no vibrato:

Teaching Example

Jackson, a tenor, is a 19-year-old sophomore vocal major at a liberal arts college in the South. He sings Tenor II in two choral ensembles: a mixed choir and a men's choir. He also auditions for any opera, musical, or play that is produced on campus, and is quite involved in extracurricular activities. He has been working with his teacher to cultivate a vibrato for several months. He is able to sing with vibrato, but inconsistently. In his lesson, he almost always sings without vibrato on slow or sustained passages of repertoire. When the voice is required to move, he is able to add more vibrancy. During the vocal exercises, he has a difficult time with consistent vibrato.

Teachers certainly don't want to discourage an enthusiastic student like Jackson from performing. However, it may be detrimental for a student of his age to do too much singing, especially in such diverse genres. Jackson may be reinforcing his non-vibrato technique by spending most of his time in various rehearsals instead of individual practice.

If he sings mainly in choir, or in an ensemble in a show, he is probably modifying his vocal technique to some degree. This modification would certainly include his vibrato rate. At some point the altered muscle memory can take over, and the straight tone will become the baseline. Therefore, he will have to work hard to cultivate his vibrato rate, which was not at all stable in the first place. Jackson may not like his voice with vibrato, especially if he has not studied voice for very long. Some beginning singers have a hard time accepting the way their vibrato sounds.

Jackson should record his lessons and monitor his progress in tandem with his teacher. His teacher can suggest specific exercises to cultivate vibrato, and Jackson should perform them in his own practice and before choral rehearsal. When he is in rehearsals of any kind, he needs to pay attention to how he is producing tone. If he can hear improved tone, with more resonance and volume, he may accept his vibrato and begin to make progress.

Notes

1. Ingo Titze, *Principles of Voice Production* (Englewood Cliffs, NJ: Prentice Hall, 1994), 337. Vibrato is understood as an ornament in singing, and is typically defined as a four-to-six-Hz undulation of pitch and intensity.

2. William Vennard, *Singing: The Mechanism and the Technic* (New York: Carl Fischer, 1968), 204.

3. Vennard, *Singing*, 206.

4. Ingo Titze, personal interview with the author, December 11, 2000.

5. Hugh Ferguson Floyd, telephone interview with the author, December 10, 2000.

6. Floyd, telephone interview.

7. Vennard, *Singing*, 206.

8. Richard Miller, *National Schools of Singing: English, French, German and Italian Techniques of Singing Revisited* (London: The Scarecrow Press, 1997), 95–97.

9. Harvey L. Woodruff, "The Choral Conductor," *The NATS Bulletin* 10 (1953): 14.

10. Floyd, telephone interview.

11. Robert T. Sataloff, "Vocal Aging and Its Medical Implications: What Singing Teachers Should Know, Part I," *Journal of Singing* 57 (2000): 29.

12. Sataloff, "Vocal Aging and Its Medical Implications," 29.

13. Sataloff, "Vocal Aging and Its Medical Implications," 32.

14. Jean Westerman Gregg, "On Voice and Age," *The NATS Journal* 47 (November–December 1990): 33.

15. Daniel R. Boone, "The Three Ages of Voice: The Singing/Acting Voice in the Mature Adult," *Journal of Voice* 11 (1997): 164.

16. Robert T. Sataloff, Deborah C. Rosen, Mary Hawkshaw, and Joseph R. Spiegel, "The Three Ages of Voice: The Aging Adult Voice," *Journal of Voice* 11 (1997): 158.

17. Richard Miller, *Solutions for Singers: Tools for Performers and Teachers* (Oxford: Oxford University Press, 2004), 237–38.

18. Martin P. Dicke, "Non-Vibrato Singing: An Historical Feature of the Performance of Early Music or a 20th Century Performance Practice Fad?" (unpublished research paper, 1999), 1–2.

19. Barbara Doscher, "Exploring the Whys of Intonation Problems," *Choral Journal* 30 (1991): 27–28.

20. Doscher, "Exploring the Whys," 28.

21. Dale Moore, "A Plea for Dialogue," *The NATS Journal* (January–February 1990): 3.

22. Barbara M. Doscher, *The Functional Unity of the Singing Voice*, 2nd ed. (London: The Scarecrow Press, 1994), 239.

23. James Luther Wrolstad, "The Effect of Choral Singing on the Developing Solo Voice" (master's thesis, California State University, Fullerton, 1979), 151.

24. Susan Sondrol Jones, personal interview with the author, November 2000.

25. Vennard, *Singing*, 2–5.

26. Richard Miller, *On the Art of Singing* (New York: Oxford University Press, 1996), 62–63.

27. Titze, personal interview.

28. Titze, personal interview.

29. Floyd, telephone interview.

30. Floyd, telephone interview.

31. Timothy Stalter, personal interview with the author, December 2000.

CHAPTER FIVE

~

Pedagogical Issues of Articulation

Articulation of Vowels and Consonants

Articulation, as it relates to diction and linguistics, can be an issue for the solo singer in the choral setting. How does a choral conductor get an entire group of people to articulate a vowel or consonant in exactly the same way at precisely the same time? While articulatory coordination of a group of singers is practically impossible to execute, it is best accomplished when singers strictly observe music's rhythmic structure and follow the conductor.

The terms "articulation," "pronunciation," and "enunciation" are sometimes used interchangeably when musicians discuss diction issues, but each term has a distinct meaning. Articulation is the movement of articulators (tongue, lips, teeth, jaw) to produce speech sounds; pronunciation is the act or result of producing speech sounds; and enunciation is the pronunciation of words in an articulate manner, or the act of speaking. These terms mean different things to different individuals, so for clarity and simplicity, the term "articulation" will be utilized in this chapter. Because text is sung on vowel sounds rather than consonant sounds, this chapter will focus principally on vowel issues.

Singers often refer to the "color," or characteristic, of a vowel sound as either bright (or forward) or dark (or back). The terms "bright" and "dark" relate to the timbre, resonance, nasality, and freedom of the tone, while the terms "forward" and "back" refer to the ease of placement of the vowel and whether it is similar in quality to the other vowels in the sung phrase. "Forward" and "back" can also reflect whether the vowel is principally formed with the tongue or the lip. For example, the vowel sounds [i] and [e] are considered front (or tongue) vowels, while the vowel sounds [o] and [u] are considered back (or lip) vowels.

In solo singing, singers can use discretion in deciding how to articulate sounds. The singer must stay within the confines of the rhythmic structure, but is free from having to coordinate with other voices. Choral singers must modify their approach to articulation to stay in sync with the conductor and group. For example, the individual choir member does not have the freedom to choose which word in the phrase to emphasize, or exactly where to place the consonants. Decisions about the ensemble's articulation are determined by the conductor, who follows the composer's intentions.

In the private studio, the student and voice teacher should remain on alert for possible developments in articulation that can result from participating in a choral ensemble. These developments include: overstating or understating initial or final consonants; releasing the diphthong too easily or not at all; incorrect foreign language diction; and loss of *legato* due to over-articulation.

In choral singing, articulation of any given vowel may prove problematic. James Jordon explains how the use of "vowel prescriptions"—vowels in the text that are demonstrated (sung) by the conductor—may not achieve the desired result:

> The choral conductor should realize that vowel prescriptions may cause a great deal of vocal damage to even the most experienced singer. At best, they are a short-term cure for a long-term problem. For example, in many choral situations, sectional "ah" vowel problems, depending on range and dynamic, may be described as "spread," "airy," "unfocused," "colorless," or "lacking resonance." Given whichever problem, the conductor issues one of a number of quick fixes for the situation. The overall sectional sound improves for an instant.[1]

In other words, each individual singer will interpret the conductor's vowel prescription in a different, and individual, way. Despite the conductor's vowel prescription, the individual's muscle memory will emerge and the vowels will not match. Singers' vocal technique is strongly integrated with their vowel formations; logically, therefore, an altered vowel means altered technique.

Ingo Titze discusses the phenomenon of group articulation of text:

> They would all have somewhat different formants. That is the amazing thing about people as you listen to them, whether they sing or speak—they can make all of the 26 or 27 phonemes in the English language differently, and yet we still recognize those phonemes. How in a chorus can we still hear, for

example, when a child and an adult female and adult male sing together—how we hear they are all singing [a] is beyond me, or anybody for that matter. Their formants are completely different, yet we hear that collectively as an [a].[2]

One reason the listener is able to understand choral diction is that consonants serve as a reference, as Titze explains:

> We hear ratios of formant frequencies and we don't know exactly whether it's an absolute formant frequency, or ratios of frequency. And sometimes we even judge the formants of the steady vowel by how you go into it and out of it. If we heard the steady section by itself, with no consonant or attack in front of it or release behind it, we wouldn't be able to define it. . . . We have taken sung vowels and excised them from the context of the text and played them for people, and people won't recognize them as human. They say, "What is this, a machine?" This is the idea of coarticulation, going from one sound to another, and it's the transition that we listen to for the clues.[3]

As Ralph D. Appleman explains, vowel modification is an essential part of any solo vocal technique:

> The teacher of *bel canto* taught the development of a vocal scale without interruption or break throughout its length. The transition of registers, while singing up or down the scale, demanded a modification of the vowel in the upper notes to preserve the true vowel sound as well as to prevent such notes from becoming disagreeable or harsh. Thus, for many centuries, teachers have used the modification of vowels as a means of transition into the upper voice.[4]

In solo technique, vowel modification—especially at the transition to the upper range—is generally considered a necessity while singing.[5] In a choral setting, however, this process might not be accepted by a conductor who is listening for a uniform vowel. Singers in the soprano and tenor sections are especially affected, as vowel modification is such an integral part of negotiating the upper register. Meanwhile, other singers in each section may not have incorporated vowel modification into their own technique.

When singers in a choral ensemble modify vowels throughout their range—whether in straight-tone singing or singing with vibrato—a non-uniform sound within the choir will result. As Hugh Ferguson Floyd has said, "Vowel modification can affect balance."[6] This can present problems for the young solo singer in the choral context. If the conductor wants a "pure vowel," then the singer could exercise the option of dropping out during the most difficult passages. Singing a high pitch without vowel modification can impede a developing young voice.

Male and female voices modify through the *passaggio* in different ways. For example, a tenor may prefer to sing more closed vowels, while a high soprano may prefer to sing more open vowels. Both of these modifications will increase comfort and enhance diction and resonance. If singers do not use vowel modification in choir, they may have difficulty modifying vowels in their solo singing. The programming of muscle memory from choral rehearsal could be substantial. The result can be overly strident tones in solo singing. A singer struggling to provide the pure vowels the conductor desires will also limit the fluctuation of his vocal folds and the vibrancy in his sound.[7]

Both choral and solo singers are likely to experience singing in a foreign language. However, the approach to learning foreign text varies from the choral setting to private studio. Vocal majors in a collegiate setting will find that training in foreign language diction is part of the curriculum. Students will likely be coached in foreign languages, and will have to spend a section of the voice lesson time on correct foreign language pronunciation. They will probably also be required to take language courses in grammar and conversation outside the music department. For the vocal major, the basis of foreign language diction study is the *International Phonetic Alphabet* (hereafter referred to as IPA). Knowledge of IPA symbols and the rules of application for each language give singers a foundation for singing in any foreign language.

A combination of intense language study and knowledge of IPA enables the vocal major to sing accurately in a foreign language. In approaching a foreign song, the process of transcribing and internalizing a foreign text is an essential step. The singer may write out the speech sounds phonetically, based on IPA, and then read over this transliteration before actually vocalizing the text. It is expected that the pitches and rhythms will be learned on given vowels before the foreign text is applied, as this process minimizes stress to the vocal mechanism.

In the choral situation, it is impossible for the conductor to listen to the foreign language pronunciation of each individual singer in the group. Moreover, unlike vocal majors, choir participants are not necessarily required to take foreign language diction and may not know IPA. The conductor's only feasible choice is to review the foreign text with the group as a whole, early in the process of learning music. Foreign pronunciation issues could also be addressed in sectional rehearsals.

The solo singer is expected to express foreign language vowels and consonants with perfect clarity, and to infuse the language with appropriate articulatory nuances. The audience's ability to understand the words, sentences, and thoughts of the solo singer is of high importance, whether the singer is performing art song, oratorio, or opera. A choral ensemble, on the other hand, produces tone and text as a group, and its singers are not judged as individuals. Audiences already have difficulty understanding any words sung by a large group of people; discerning a text sung by a group in a foreign language is even more challenging. Is it possible for a group of people, most of whom speak English as a first language, to pronounce a mixed German vowel the exact same way? Since no two people pronounce a pure vowel the same way, it is highly unlikely that a large chorus can enunciate a mixed vowel (two vowel sounds pronounced at the same time) en masse.

Perhaps the best way for a choral conductor to convey foreign language text to a group is through repetition of example rather than IPA. An argument can be made that the use of IPA is not necessary in the choral environment. Brenda Smith and Robert Sataloff explain how they believe a chorus should learn a foreign text:

> Choral singers learn to sing texts in foreign languages by imitation and repetition. It is generally not time-effective to expect choral singers to learn the International Phonetic Alphabet as their tool for pronunciation. Some zealous choir members may want to include the symbols in their own factual baggage, but most will find it an impediment. Instead, the choir must rely on good examples spoken and sung by the conductor or a language assistant.[8]

Even if the choral and solo approaches to learning foreign language differ, singers and conductors can surely agree that the text of a song or choral work is fundamental to the success of performance. The text is an integral part of the choral composer's conception, and the singer's textual awareness must be raised for meaningful interpretation to occur.

The solo singer will want to remain self-aware in choir when it comes to foreign language text and the rules of diction. A choral conductor who introduces IPA concepts and symbols in the choral ensemble is benefitting solo singers by reinforcing what they are learning in the studio. If for some reason the conductor does not focus on pronunciation, solo singers should be their own primary resource when preparing the text.

Issues and Solutions

ISSUE: Text emphasis is an individual choice for the solo singer, but in the choral setting, the singer cannot choose which words and syllables to emphasize in a given phrase. The choral ensemble must choose points of textual emphasis according to the demands of the literature as interpreted by the conductor.

SOLUTION: Singers in choral rehearsal can look at this issue in a positive light, as an opportunity to practice following a conductor and applying his vision of text interpretation. When singing art songs, singers have control over text emphasis. However, in opera or as a soloist in *oratorio* or symphonic works, singers occasionally have to be led by the conductor in this matter.

ISSUE: Not all singers in a choral ensemble will pronounce foreign language diction correctly or in the same manner.

SOLUTION: Singers can only be responsible for their own pronunciations. They can make diction markings in their scores with correct IPA symbols and write out any challenging words in complete IPA transliteration. When singing in German or French, singers in choir rehearsal have a great opportunity to practice the pronunciation of mixed and nasal vowels such as ü, ö, ã and ũn. IPA rules can be reviewed during choir rehearsal and singers can refer to a dictionary with IPA symbols. As young singers learn new IPA symbols in diction courses, they can give IPA concepts special attention in choral rehearsal to reinforce their learning.

ISSUE: Vowel prescriptions given by the conductor may not be the ideal way for singers to articulate a vowel. No two people form a vowel in exactly the same manner. The articulators shape resonance into vowels, and articulators vary from person to person.

SOLUTION: Singers should try to match the conductor's vowel to the best of their ability. For example, if the conductor asks the choir to collectively darken an [a] vowel, the singer does not have to shift placement of the vowel or change the resonating space (pharynx) in a substantial manner. The conductor is probably asking for a less bright vowel, and singers can respond by backing off their forward placement slightly, altering to an open "o," or lowering the dynamic. The basic idea is to give the conductor what he wants without completely changing voice production.

ISSUE: The conductor's desire for a uniform vowel above the staff may exceed the comfort level for singers. For example, if the sopranos are singing an [i] sound on a G5, the most comfortable modification may be to an [i] sound, but the conductor might prefer that the sopranos keep the [i] vowel above the staff.

SOLUTION: Singers should try to keep the vowel as authentic as possible while modifying for a comfortable tone. Visualizing the phonetic symbol of the vowel in question may be helpful. Also, making notes in the score will help singers vocally anticipate these vowels in performance.

ISSUE: The conductor may not use IPA symbols in choral rehearsal when teaching foreign language literature.

SOLUTION: Even if the conductor does not use IPA symbols, solo singers should practice IPA in the choral ensemble to supplement their foreign language study. Singers can take pronunciation cues from the conductor and write them down in phonetic symbols. This practice of symbol usage will benefit singers in future teaching or performance. It is more professional to use IPA symbols rather than vernacular letters in solo or choral rehearsal.

Issue: When singing in a foreign language in choir, singers risk using incorrect pronunciation and forming bad diction habits.

Solution: If singers in choir are unsure of the correct foreign language pronunciation, they can consult dictionaries and diction textbooks or listen to reputable recordings. During a break in rehearsal, they can ask the conductor questions related to diction, or consult with other members of the ensemble.

Vowel Clarity Exercises

Vowel Clarity Exercise 1

Singers move up and down by half steps, within their comfort level, singing a series of five vowel sounds. Make sure every vowel is distinctive from the others. Also make sure to articulate each vowel correctly, without unconsciously modifying it to a different sound. Check yourself by recording your practice, and also have a friend listen. Don't tell the friend which vowels you are singing; ask the friend to write the vowels down and read them back to you.

Vowel Clarity Exercise 2

Singers move up by half steps and then back down, singing each vowel clearly, moving from open to closed vowels, and feeling the formation of each vowel:

Vowel Clarity Exercise for Lip Vowels

Sing in whichever range is comfortable. The important thing is to sing the exact vowel indicated by the IPA symbol. Repeated practice will help solidify the articulatory position for each vowel sound and increase muscle memory, so that clarity is present when text is added to these vowels:

va   va   va_____   vo   vo   vo_____

vɔ   vɔ   vɔ_____   vu   vu   vu_____

Vowel Clarity Exercise for Tongue Vowels

Follow instructions for "Vowel Clarity Exercise for Lip Vowels," above:

ve   ve   ve_____   vɛ   vɛ   vɛ_____   vi   vi   vi_____

Teaching Example

Greg, a baritone, is a 25-year-old graduate student at a liberal arts college in the Northeast. He is an extremely bright student with a strong interest in languages and speech science. He lived abroad for several years with his family, and is fluent in Italian and French. He is in a large ensemble that includes undergraduates, graduates, and some singers who are not music majors.

Since joining this large choral ensemble, he has noticed that some of the singers do not sing the correct vowel and consonant sounds when singing in French. He also notices that when the conductor gives the ensemble pronunciation corrections, the choir members do not mark the changes in their score.

Greg takes a survey of choral literature course with the conductor. Thus Greg has observed firsthand that the conductor has substantial knowledge of foreign languages. In rehearsal the conductor has taken care to practice the difficult sounds of French with the group, but Greg observes that the singers are still not correctly pronouncing the sounds.

Greg sings the foreign language with the correct pronunciation, which is at odds with the sounds produced by other singers. For example, he is correctly pronouncing nasal vowels, while the others are not including any nasality in these vowels. These clashing sounds are causing some friction in his section. He has tried to correct singers sitting near him, but this has not been well-received.

The solo singer is used to having control over his performance, including the beauty of the tone and the accuracy of the language. In a group situation, the individual cannot control other people.

Because of his fluency in foreign languages, Greg has a unique contribution to make to the group. He can speak to the conductor about improving the French of the group, and offer a suggestion: the conductor could set aside some time to rehearse French during the sectional rehearsals. This could be a valuable teaching experience for Greg, since he is a graduate student and older than many of the students, and others would benefit as well. Greg's case illustrates how a conductor can utilize members of his choir in a practical and effective way.

Differences in the Choral and Solo Approach to Diction

In contrast to solo work, the discipline of choral singing requires more of a group approach to dealing with language. For example, in chorus *precision* is the primary factor in making a vowel sound, whereas in solo singing, producing as *authentic* a vowel sound as possible is paramount.

In the choral ensemble, when singing in German or French, a mixed vowel must be articulated in the exact same manner by a group of people. Since no two people articulate a vowel sound the same way, this can be difficult! Soloists pronounce mixed vowels as individuals and have the freedom to focus on the color of the vowel rather than coordination with other singers.

When a choral ensemble sings a diphthong (two consecutive vowel sounds), the timing must be coordinated by the conductor. The easiest way to sing a diphthong as a group is to divide the two vowel sounds by the rhythmic structure of the measure. A soloist, on the other hand, can freely execute diphthongs without having to consider other singers. In solo singing, a diphthong is most often executed by extending the first vowel and shortening the second. For words that contain diphthongs, solo singers can focus on dramatic interpretation without the constriction of group unity.

In the choral setting, plosive consonants such as [b], [p], and [k] have to come *before* the beat of the measure in which they are written in order for the group to coordinate the placement and pitch. Soloists are not restricted by this coordination, and can use plosive consonants to emphasize certain words and dramatic ideas.

Final consonants are often the most important letters of the word, and their pronunciation is critical to understanding choral and solo texts. In the chorus, final consonants must be coordinated by every member of the group in order for the audience to understand the text. In solo singing, an individual has the option of using final consonants to emphasize certain words, create dramatic context, and wield the voice expressively.

Groupings of consonants (consonant clusters) can cause some confusion in the choral ensemble. A very common instance is "gl," as in the word "gloria." A solo singer's instinct is to sing quickly through the cluster straight to the open "o" vowel. In the choral ensemble, on the other hand, singers are often encouraged to linger on the first, or even second, consonant of the cluster for emphasis, or in an effort to coordinate the ensemble. As any singer knows, sustaining tone on a consonant is challenging.

As mentioned earlier, vowel modification is common in both solo and choral singing and necessary for vocal health, but not every singer modifies vowels in the same manner. For example, each member of a soprano section singing G5 above the staff will modify a sung vowel according to her own concept of vowel articulation and her unique use of articulators (tongue, lips, jaw, and palates). If each soprano's modified vowels were isolated and recorded, each would be heard articulating a different vowel. Perhaps the best that conductors and singers can hope for is to keep the integrity of the original vowel when singing.

Choral diction in Latin raises some special considerations. For example, depending on the composer, conductors may temper their textual interpretation with German- or French-influenced Latin rather than the basic Ecclesiastical Latin used by most soloists. These alternate pronunciations are not always based on clear rules, and are often derived from recordings, which may or may not be accurate. It is up to the conductor to convey the most precise pronunciation possible.

Notes

1. James M. Jordon, "False Blend: A Vocal Pedagogy Problem for the Choral Conductor," *Choral Journal* 24 (1984): 26.

2. Ingo Titze, personal interview with the author, December 11, 2000.

3. Titze, personal interview.

4. Ralph D. Appleman, *The Science of Vocal Pedagogy: Theory and Application* (Bloomington: Indiana University Press, 1967), 220–21.

5. Barbara M. Doscher, *The Functional Unity of the Singing Voice*, 2nd ed. (London: The Scarecrow Press, 1994), 145.

6. Hugh Ferguson Floyd, telephone interview with the author, November 10, 2000.

7. Doscher, *The Functional Unity*, 193.

8. Brenda Smith and Robert T. Sataloff, *Choral Pedagogy* (San Diego: Singular Publishing Group, 2000), 154.

CHAPTER SIX

~

Pedagogical Issues of Classification, Blend, Rehearsal Demands, and Tone Quality: Expectations of the Choral Conductor

Choral conductors are in a position to positively or negatively influence solo singers in their ensemble. Choral conductor Lloyd Pfautsch offers his belief that the choral environment should complement and enhance solo study:

> Although vocal training provided by choral conductors is somewhat different from that which singers receive in private studios, the technique employed in rehearsal should always be compatible with that used in the private studio.[1]

Preferences in voice classification, blend, rehearsal demands, and tone quality are among the most important pedagogical issues a conductor must handle.

Voice Classification

The proper classification of the voice is essential to vocal health in both the voice studio and choral environment. The method and outcome of classification differ greatly in these two contexts. A choral singer is usually classified as one of four principal parts: soprano, alto, tenor, or bass. Within these parts are variations of high and low (Soprano I and Soprano II, for example). The collegiate solo singer interested in a professional career will be working toward a voice classification based on the *fach* system, a German classification system for operatic voices. Young singers will identify with lyric categories, and with age and additional training will later refine these categories to include classifications such as dramatic or *coloratura*.[2]

During the choral audition process a choral conductor has only a few minutes to assess a voice for classification. This classification will be applied for a minimum of one semester. If a student's voice is going through vocal changes, the choral conductor can help by being willing to consider changing parts mid-semester. The solo singer and voice teacher spend years developing the voice, and the classification may change with time and experience. In most cases, at the end of undergraduate work (age 21 or 22), the solo singer will need three or four more years of formal training before the *fach* category is determined.

The choral conductor must make the choral classification himself, even when the solo singer has sought the input of teachers and professional opera coaches over a period of several years. Some choral conductors will confer with voice teachers before classification. This is beneficial for the vocal health of the student, and helps create a productive work environment for all faculty.

Misclassification of a young singer is a common occurrence, as James McKinney explains:

> The typical choral situation affords many opportunities for misclassification to occur. The most common division of vocal parts is for high and low voices within each sex (SATB). Since most people have medium voices, they must be assigned to a part which is either too high or too low for them; the *mezzo-soprano* must sing soprano and the baritone must sing tenor or bass. Either option can present problems for the singer, but for most singers there are fewer dangers in singing too low than there are in singing too high.[3]

The choral conductor will be listening for a singer's timbre, range, negotiation of *passaggio* (transition points), and overall vocal health. The ultimate decision of singer placement also depends on the choral conductor's specifications for section balance.

For example, Timothy Stalter explains that "most women are moving upward during the developmental collegiate years."[4] This may result in the misclassification of young sopranos. Young sopranos are frequently placed in the alto section to fill it out, as most women are not true altos. A soprano with excellent sight-reading skills or a particularly warm timbre combined with a lower-pitched voice can add much to the alto section, but this move may work against the development of the solo singer. As Titze states:

> It is particularly tough for the mezzo-sopranos and tenors because they are messing around in the *passaggio* region, and they are dealing with registration problems. They're always pitched right in the crack (D4 to F#4). The

sopranos will also get down in there, but are well enough above the *primo passaggio*. If a singer hasn't learned a technique, especially with a medium loud voice, the singer will strangle himself. He'll push it up . . . or he will go to a falsetto sound.[5]

Stalter discusses his procedure for classification:

Range is not the sole determinant factor. . . . Are they able to negotiate the *passaggio*? I also listen to the timbre—is it a high, light timbre? I find very few true altos. I want to know who they are studying with, and I will call the teacher to see if they agree—consultation with the teacher is important.[6]

Hugh Ferguson Floyd also emphasizes consultation with students and voice teachers:

I encourage students to talk to me and not to feel stuck. Misclassification can be very dangerous. . . . I have pivot singers who switch parts from piece to piece for more comfortable vocal production.[7]

The use of *pivot singers* is an excellent option for choral classification, as this will reduce stress on the vocal mechanism and prevent the student from singing in an uncomfortable *tessitura* for too long. Active communication among singer, conductor, and voice teacher is the logical approach to serving the interests of all parties. All three parties should strive for the same goal of healthy vocal production.

Issues and Solutions

Issue: A singer auditioning for an ensemble can be misclassified for a number of reasons.

Solution: Singers who are uncomfortable with their assigned parts in choir should change parts after consulting with their voice teacher and the conductor of the ensemble. Misclassification can manifest itself in excessive vocal fatigue, diminishing range (high or low), hoarseness in the speaking and singing voice, and loss of vocal stamina.

Issue: Very few professional female singers are mezzo-sopranos, just as very few female voice students are mezzo-sopranos. Therefore, filling the alto section of an ensemble is a challenge for every conductor. Sopranos are often placed in the alto section.

Solution: If a soprano whose top comfortable pitch is G5 is assigned an Alto I part in an ensemble, this may not be a detriment to her technique.

She should be careful not to get too heavy below C4, and she can use the experience to strengthen her middle and low registers. A tenor with limited high pitches would be at a much greater disadvantage if he were placed in the bass section. He would be singing much lower than he ever would in solo literature. It is very common for a young soprano or tenor not to have the high extension required in the most challenging choral literature. How can a singer handle this situation? Perhaps the best solution is Hugh Ferguson Floyd's idea of a pivot singer. A pivot singer's voice does not perfectly fit into a choral classification, but can change parts as needed for vocal comfort. If singers recognize when they do not fit into a classification, and they can speak with the conductor about pivot singing.

Issue: Young singers will not be ready to finalize their voice classification in the collegiate years.

Solution: In both the solo and choral environments, it is perfectly acceptable for singers to change voice classification throughout the maturation process. Singers should sing the most appropriate repertoire for them, and avoid any *tessitura* that causes discomfort.

How to Tell If You Are Misclassified in Choral Ensemble
1. You notice vocal fatigue during and after chorus on a regular basis, but not during or after a voice lesson.
2. The *tessitura* you are singing in feels uncomfortable on a regular basis, and does not seem to fit your voice.
3. The other singers in your section are singing significantly different solo repertoire than you are.
4. Your voice has changed significantly since you auditioned for the conductor, and you are now singing much higher or lower repertoire than before.
5. You are losing the ability to clearly phonate in the top or bottom range of your voice, or you cannot vocalize comfortably at the very top or bottom of your range in practice sessions.
6. Your teacher has mentioned that your range seems more restricted, or that you are singing too heavily in a certain range.
7. Solo repertoire that was once comfortable and easy now seems difficult.
8. Your instincts tell you that you are in the incorrect section!

Teaching Example

Joseph, a tenor, is a 20-year-old junior in a small ensemble at a conservatory in the South. He has a small-sized voice and feels very comfortable singing light lyric tenor literature. He sings the Tenor I part in his choral ensemble. In voice lessons, Joseph's teacher has been working with him on singing with his full voice at the very top of his voice. Joseph is just beginning to feel comfortable with this concept, and spends a few minutes of private practice each day on exercises that stretch his top voice.

Since focusing on this aspect of his technique, he has noticed that he is extremely fatigued after choir rehearsal each day. He is very concerned, especially since his private practice and lessons have been going so well.

Joseph has been singing the Tenor I part in choir with a basically unsupported tone on the upper pitches. This has worked well for him in terms of "fitting in" with the rest of the section and not feeling conspicuous. But now that his top voice is coming into its own and he is practicing every day, he is finding it more and more difficult to modify his top voice in the choral ensemble. He is singing full voice in his practice and lessons, and half voice, or marking, in choir. Now that his voice is conditioned to sing with abdominal support, he fatigues more quickly when it is not supported.

For Joseph in chorus, dynamic variation in the top voice is a particular challenge. He is not technically able to handle the challenging messa di voce in the top voice. So instead of trying to sing softly during those passages, he simply disconnects his abdominal engagement and sings from the throat.

Joseph is at a delicate stage in his development. He is coordinating his technique for the top voice, but is not yet able to add nuance. He wants to sing as a soloist, so he must not back away from the progress he is making in his solo work. If he feels comfortable with his conductor, he might ask something along the lines of, "Professor Smith, I have been trying something new with my top voice, do you mind if I sing that way today?" It may be that the conductor prefers Joseph's full voice to his unsupported one.

His teacher could suggest that Joseph switch to Tenor II while he works out the top voice in his lessons. Another idea is for Joseph to practice the most difficult passages of the score in full voice, and then sing the passages that way in rehearsal, seeing if the conductor has any objection.

As Joseph matures physically, he should be able to add dynamic variation to his technique.

Choral Blend

Solo singers in the choral setting are required to find a balance between the technique they utilize in choir and the technique they utilize in solo work. If solo singers were to participate in an ensemble with their usual intensity, vibrancy, and breath patterns, they would most certainly stand out. Common courtesy, tradition, and the expectations of the conductor require that most singers participate in ensembles as members of a group, not soloists. By necessity, this participation will require some modification of the individual vocal technique.

The term *blend* is often associated with choral aesthetics, but choral conductors have expressed uncertainty about this word. Timothy Stalter says "blend is a slippery word,"[8] and Hugh Ferguson Floyd states, "There is no such thing as blend—blend is a cooking term." Floyd prefers the concept of "balanced volume level."[9]

In their book *Choral Pedagogy*, Smith and Sataloff outline the components of blended sound:

1. Color: no individual voices are identifiable. Also, a distinct sound quality typifies each section and the whole choir.
2. Balance: individual choral sections are balanced within the tonal texture.
3. Tuning: voice leading is accurate, resolving points of tension clearly, and pitch is accurate and consistent among sections.
4. Diction: vowels and consonants are pronounced uniformly and can be understood by an audience.[10]

By stating that blend is accomplished when "no individual voices are identifiable," Smith and Sataloff provide the solo singer with a reason to avoid choral singing. As James Wrolstad warns, "By modifying the vocal technique in order to blend, the solo singer is denying his true voice and diminishing its quality."[11]

As Johan Sundberg explains, spectral analysis has revealed how voices are modified in a choral setting:

Goodwin compared how sopranos used their voices when they sang to create a choral blend and when they sang as soloists. Spectral analysis revealed not only that the singers sang more loudly but also that the overtones were louder when they performed as soloists. In the case of the male subjects, pairs of tones sung at the same pitch, on the same vowel and with the same loudness in both experimental settings were compared; in the solo situation, each singer had a louder singer formant and slightly softer overtones below about 500 Hz. Also, the singers adapted the loudness more closely to that of the earphone reference in the case of choral singing.[12]

This scientific investigation underlines of importance of singers monitoring their technique for signs of modification in the choral environment. In solo singing, the ability to produce an overtone series is what enables the singer's voice to carry over an orchestra and obtain the ring essential to individual vocal color and audience perception.

A scientific study by Allen Goodwin, entitled "An Acoustical Study of Individual Voices in Choral Blend," has also demonstrated that the solo voice can be severely altered in a choral setting. Goodwin concluded that "blended vocal tones tended to have fewer and weaker partials [overtones] on frequencies above the first formant." He went on to explain that "for tones produced in the blending situation, the second and third formants had proportionately lower levels of intensity than were present in the solo singer." He also compared how sopranos sang as soloists to how they used their voices to create a choral blend. When they performed as soloists, the spectral analysis showed that they sang more loudly, and with louder overtones.[13] Overtones are highly desirable to solo singers and are reduced when singers modify their technique to blend.

Goodwin believes that this loss of intensity and vibrancy has a direct effect on a singer's vibrato rate: "Singers whose vocal tones had strong or numerous upper partials tended to reduce that vibrato extent slightly . . . when attempting to blend."[14] In short, singers must realize that their intensity, vibrancy, and vibrato rate will probably lessen while participating in choir. Knowing this, the singer should be able to regain these traits when singing alone.

Choral conductors face the challenge of helping many voices balance with each other. Timothy Stalter speaks of his personal experience with Robert Shaw, and Shaw's method of promoting blend:

> Shaw seated people according to timbre. The highest, lightest tenor would sit next to, in a circle, the lowest, darkest tenor, next to the highest, lightest baritone, to the lowest, darkest bass, which would dovetail to the highest, lightest soprano, etc. We rehearsed in a circle, and for performance we would stand in two semicircles. . . . There is something to be said about people learning to listen to others.[15]

Stalter makes an important point here. One advantage of young singers blending in choir is the chance to learn how to listen to others. Any soloist performing a duet, trio, or quartet will need to learn about factors of balance.

Not every choral conductor agrees on what blend encompasses, and some strive for a more individualistic choral sound. Paul Peterson explains:

> In regard to the problem of developing a good choral blend, we have one of the most controversial subjects among choir directors today. Some directors base their selection of singers on their ability to imitate a tone he considers

an ideal. It may take the form of a straight tone, white, dark, dramatic, or any other tonal effect. By this method, each voice is molded to fit this imitational quality and the choir is deprived of its true natural beauty and richness of tone. Rather than imitation, we should strive for the results obtained by the use of beautiful sustained speech which is the basis for good singing.[16]

This statement, written back in 1952 at a Southeastern National Association of Teachers of Singing (NATS) conference, is remarkably ahead of its time; many choral conductors would say the same thing today. From the same remarks:

A consideration of blending trained and untrained voices is most familiar to . . . the college director attempting to blend voices of piano and voice majors. The choir director has two choices—either to subdue the trained voices to blend with the others, or, develop the untrained singers into a higher degree of performance to blend with the solo voices. No doubt, we all agree to the latter plan.[17]

This opinion reflects the feelings of choral conductors from the past and present. Many choral conductors seriously consider the needs of the solo voice when conceptualizing the blend of their ensemble. This is good news for the solo singer.

Issues and Solutions

ISSUE: Singing in a choral ensemble calls for "blend" or "balanced volume level," both of which requires modification for the solo singer. Regular modification of the vocal technique in a choral setting can change the solo technique.

SOLUTION: One option for a solo singer is to participate in a *small* vocal ensemble. A group of eight to sixteen singers might require less blending on the part of individuals. Singers could be more assertive and independent vocally, staying closer to the technique they use in a solo setting or an opera chorus.

SOLUTION: Vocalizing before and immediately following choral rehearsal helps singers counterbalance the modification in choral rehearsal with their solo technique.

ISSUE: Solo singers are distinctive, and individuality is critical to their professional success. Choral singing requires that singers restrain their individuality.

SOLUTION: For this reason, a young singer with great vocal promise and in possession of a truly unique instrument might not even want to participate in choral singing. Such singers can attend an academic institution where choral singing is not a requirement for the vocal major.

Issue: Individual resonance, rich with overtones, is essential for solo singers to carry their voice above an orchestra. However, individual resonance is not cultivated in choir.

Solution: Singing a lower voice part may allow singers to employ more of their full acoustic load in choral rehearsal. Singers should also spend more time in the practice room than in choir rehearsal to combat the dampening effect that choral work has on their overtone series. A singer can also try singing full voice in choir. The conductor's reaction may be favorable!

Issue: Scientific evidence has demonstrated that singers attempting to blend in choir reduce their vibrato rate.

Solution: Singers should strive to keep their vibrato rate intact during choral rehearsal by lowering the intensity of their dynamics but not the intensity of their vocal energy or abdominal connection.

Teaching Example

Antoine, a bass-baritone, is a 23-year-old senior at a liberal arts college in the South. He is a member of a collegiate choir that has many performances each semester and rehearses several times per week. In recent lessons, Antoine's teacher has noticed that his breath energy seems low and his vibrato is often diminished. His overall vocal quality is lacking its usual vibrancy, color, and energy.

Antoine's lack of vocal energy and vibrancy may result from the demands of his choral ensemble, or his lack of individual practice, or—most likely—a combination of the two. He may be physically and vocally tired, or vocally out of shape!

If a student singer has an obligation to a busy ensemble, individual practice can easily lose priority. It is the responsibility of singers to put their individual practice first. Singers must find time to vocalize on a regular basis and practice their repertoire. Singers must also sustain good vocal technique when singing in an ensemble, just as they do when singing as soloists.

Antoine needs to find a way to balance his solo work with his choral obligations, and to work practice into his daily life. With some attention paid to his breath energy and vibrato rate, and a restored sense of balance, Antoine should start sounding better very soon.

Teaching Example

Holly, a soprano, is a 26-year-old graduate student in her second semester of study at a Midwestern university. She has a uniquely large-sized instrument. Her teacher is planning on Holly's participation in the upcoming Metropolitan Opera regional auditions, and is focusing on literature by Verdi, Wagner, and Leoncavallo. At her audition for choir in the fall (a requirement for every vocal major), the conductor placed her in the alto section, after discussing the matter with her voice teacher. He explained that because of her distinctive voice, the alto section was the best place for her to blend.

As the semester has progressed, Holly has felt increasingly self-conscious in choral rehearsal. She wants to participate as a member of the group, but her colleagues in the alto section frequently comment on the size of her voice. The conductor has asked Holly to "hold back" her sound several times, and often looks in her direction whenever the alto section has an exposed musical passage.

Holly may be one of the few people who really cannot blend into a choral ensemble. Because of her large-sized voice, vocal maturity, and distinctive vocal timbre, she is different from other singers her age. The question becomes: how can faculty best deal with a unique singer like Holly and still be fair to other singers who have a choral requirement for their degree? There needs to be some kind of dispensation for a professional-caliber singer like Holly, who does not fit into an ensemble.

Demands Placed on the Singer during Choral Rehearsal

The choral rehearsal demands addressed in this section encompass four categories: repetition, volume control, duration, and vocal energy. Repetition in choral singing refers to repeating any given phrase at the conductor's request. The conductor may request repetition to instill a vocal color preference, or to improve rhythmic accuracy, diction, or intonation. Some choral conductors are aware that frequent repetition can have unanticipated consequences. Choral conductor Lloyd Pfautsch refers to unnecessary repetition as a "pitfall" for conductors: "The music is repeated over and over with benevolent allowances for mistakes in the hope that increased familiarity will eventually eliminate the mistakes."[18]

Repetition can contribute to fatigue, which may be exacerbated if the singer becomes frustrated. It is impossible to measure the usefulness of repetition exercises for each individual choir member. Singers may not even know if they are making an error, since they likely cannot hear themselves. If singers have checked their rhythmic accuracy, diction, and pitches, and believe they are singing correctly—while their voices tire out from multiple repetitions—they may opt to drop out and discontinue repeating the given phrase.

Volume control can also be an issue for the solo singer in choir. Because of the sound from other voices, singers cannot gauge their volume level as accurately as they can when singing alone. Singing softly in choir may cause the singer's abdominal musculature to be less engaged than it should. Singers may also be oversinging and taxing the vocal mechanism for long periods of time when the conductor calls for a more full sound. If singers are feeling excessive fatigue or hoarseness after a choral rehearsal, lack of volume control—either from oversinging or undersinging—may be a cause. It is therefore extremely important that singers consistently remind themselves to engage their abdominal musculature and support the tone fully at all times when singing in choir.

The duration of the choral rehearsal can affect a singer's vocal output for the rest of the day. A typical collegiate choral rehearsal can last anywhere from fifty minutes to two hours. Choral conductors will not typically require every singer to sing actively throughout the entire rehearsal. Conductors may spend time with one section or discuss issues related to the music. Solo singers can utilize this time to follow along in their music and increase their knowledge of the musical style and diction.

The more thoroughly singers know their part, the less vocally taxing it will be to sing. In deciding how much vocal effort to devote to choral rehearsal, singers should consider the style of the music as well as how much additional singing they must do that day. If students have completed their private practice before choir and do not have to sing for the rest of the day, they might feel comfortable singing throughout the entire choral rehearsal. However, singers who have additional performing commitments and have yet to practice might want to "save" their voices for those activities. This is not ideal for the conductor, but he should empathize with the demands of the vocal major and be willing to accommodate those commitments.

It is not reasonable to expect an undergraduate vocal major to sing more than two hours each day. Scientific studies have examined the effects of prolonged phonation time on the voice. As Titze writes,

> Accumulated phonation time has been measured. Holbrook, for example, reported that twelve elementary school teachers during a six-hour contact period with children had an average of seventy-seven minutes of total phonation time. Twenty minutes of this was phonation above 75 dBA [decibels], . . . a condition he called loud phonation. . . . Accumulated phonation time by itself is clearly not a predictor of vocal fatigue . . . intensity and fundamental frequency must be factored in . . . but what about all the vocal stops and starts? And what about the differences in the sound quality produced? This problem becomes more like predicting the fatigue of a football player on the basis of the number of sprints, collisions, lunges and tackles in a game . . . more acoustic dimensions need to be probed to establish reliable predictors of vocal fatigue.[19]

Holbrook's study pertains to non-singers, of course, but the loud phonation of teachers can certainly be compared to singers in terms of effort and effect on the voice.

When planning college curriculum requirements, vocal and choral faculty should work with administrative faculty to design a schedule conducive to the development of young voices. As Leon Thurman writes, "On the day of a choral concert, it would be best for the choral conductor to avoid a full rehearsal before performance as this will fatigue voices (already tired at the end of the day) so they have nothing left for performance."[20]

The idea of *vocal energy* relates to how much voice a vocal major is expected to devote to choral rehearsal. If undergraduates have a choral rehearsal for one-and-a-half hours twice a week, then for those two days, most of their vocal energy will be spent in choir. Typical vocal majors will be required to sing in several classes a week, including private lessons. Their teachers should advise them on how best to expend their vocal energy.

Any unrealistic expectations by faculty that young students can produce sound for several hours each day will only result in vocal fatigue, ineffective practice, and frustration for the singer. Discussion and exploration of choral alternatives such as participation in a smaller ensemble or a conducting choir (an ensemble made up of students to provide conducting experience for another student) could be beneficial.

The neglected issue of vocal energy deserves more discussion and attention from music associations and societies as well as music faculty. Unrealistic expectations of voice majors, in terms of how much time they should devote to singing each day, can cause stress and diminished performance quality within a music department.

Issues and Solutions

ISSUE: In the choral ensemble, singers may be asked to repeat a musical phrase many times in a row. This repetition may not have anything to do with the quality of an individual's singing. In other words, singers may be using their voices for no purpose other than to correct another singer's vocal or musical issues.

SOLUTION: The conductor is at a disadvantage in this situation. In the group environment, conductors cannot always ascertain which individual is singing incorrectly. Therefore, to make improvements, they have to ask the entire section to repeat certain phrases. Singers should sing the phrase as requested, but they should have the choice not to continue when it becomes obvious that no improvements are forthcoming. It is not realistic to expect a group of people to sing repetitively so that the mistakes of one or two people can be corrected.

ISSUE: Modification of dynamic levels during the rehearsal can greatly affect the solo technique of any singer, as they are inextricably linked together. Singers reducing their volume level consistently in a rehearsal are likely to fatigue.

SOLUTION: Singers should do their best to accommodate the requests of the conductor. They may not be able to maintain modification of the dynamic levels, but should sing for as long as they can. If singers can no longer maintain the volume control requested and feel fatigue or discomfort, they should stop singing immediately.

ISSUE: The duration of the choral rehearsal can fatigue singers and greatly affect their ability to sing for the rest of the day.

SOLUTION: Because singers can only sing for a certain amount of time each day, it is wise for them to plan choral singing into their weekly schedule. Voice faculty and choral conductors need to be realistic about the expectations demanded of singers. If a voice teacher requires two hours of applied practice each day, and the regular chorus rehearsal is ninety minutes each day, that is too much singing for an undergraduate. Singers should always fit in their daily individual practice first. Some singers do not like singing in the morning, but this ensures that private practice happens each day. Solo practice and lesson preparation should be the primary focus for any vocal major. If singers have additional singing after choral rehearsal, such as church singing or opera rehearsal, then they should probably not sing in choir rehearsal. Singers should take care to fulfill their obligations to choral rehearsal as much as possible, so that on occasions when they need to "save" or rest their voices, the conductor will be understanding.

ISSUE: Choral conductors like to rehearse the day of a concert or performance. Some conductors will even call a full rehearsal on the same day as a performance. Most solo singers prefer to conserve their voices on performance days, except for a small amount of vocalizing.

SOLUTION: The ideal scenario is for choral conductors to strictly limit the amount of rehearsal time on a performance day, vocalizing the ensemble immediately before the concert and spending less than fifteen minutes rehearsing specific passages in the music. If a rehearsal extends longer, singers can conserve their voices by using half voice or marking in rehearsal, and then singing full voice in the performance. Another strategy is to sing only half the amount of repertoire in rehearsal. This is a case in which singers and conductor meeting each other halfway will result in both happier singers and a better concert.

How to Handle the Vocal Demands of Choir

1. Combat fatigue by drinking plenty of water before, during, and after rehearsal.
2. In spare moments, silently study your choral scores to better familiarize yourself with the repertoire, so that your voice is not overworking to learn the notes in rehearsal.
3. Remember all the aspects of healthy technique during rehearsal. Always keep the abdominal muscles engaged. Breathe low, slow, and silently. When you cannot hear yourself, use your senses to sing. Sit tall to allow room for the rib cage to expand.
4. Do not try to vocally compensate for other singers in the section that are undersinging—this is an impossible task.
5. Avoid sitting near singers who are unnecessarily loud and talk during rehearsal.
6. When you have many singing obligations during a particular week, learn how to conserve your voice in choir by marking or not singing at all—at least for part of rehearsal.
7. If a combination of dynamics and *tessitura* is too demanding, do not sing.
8. Genuinely learn to enjoy the choral experience!

Teaching Example

Taiko, a tenor, is a 22-year-old vocal major at a university in the Northeast. He has always enjoyed singing in choir, and recently moved to the most demanding ensemble on campus. Lately, after choir rehearsal, he notices that he is hoarse and unable to phonate easily. At the beginning of the semester, this only happened a few times, but as the semester has progressed, Taiko has lost his voice more and more often. As a result he is unable to sing in studio class, applied lessons, and other performance situations.

Clearly Taiko's vocal issues, whatever they may be, have been exacerbated by the demands of his new choral ensemble. This student may have more than one severe problem with his technique. If he is regularly losing his voice completely, there may be concerns with his physical health.

If Taiko has any physical symptoms of illness, he should consult a doctor as soon as possible. Many students experience an onset of certain illnesses in early adulthood. Undiagnosed allergies, sleep apnea, and acid reflux are just a few of the problems that can cause vocal trauma.

If physical problems are ruled out, Taiko might benefit from switching in choir to a different part where he uses mostly his middle voice. Avoiding the extreme ends of his range while he works out his vocal problems is probably wise. Also, as a tempo-rary measure, Taiko can talk to his conductor about resting his voice occasionally in rehearsal, perhaps for five full minutes every half hour.

Teaching Example

Teresa, a soprano, is a 19-year-old freshman vocal major at a college in the South. She is singing Soprano I in the largest ensemble on campus. Most of her vocal major colleagues are in a smaller ensemble, but Teresa chose the bigger ensemble because she really likes the conductor and the ensemble's repertoire. She has many singing obligations coming up, including a solo performance with the jazz band, performances of opera scenes, a monthly departmental recital, preparations for her jury, and two important choral concerts. In addition, she has a weekly voice lesson and studio class.

When her teacher hears hoarseness in Teresa's speaking voice for the third week in a row, and learns of all of her singing obligations, she suggests that Teresa drop one or two of her commitments. Teresa responds that she wants to keep all of them.

Teresa's voice is most definitely overextended. Even though she enjoys the larger ensemble, she may benefit greatly from a smaller group. Singers tend to cultivate greater awareness of their own voice in smaller ensembles.

Singers like Teresa need to realize that some semesters will be busier than others. Singing obligations, like life obligations, need to be balanced in a way that allows for healthy singing. For example, even though Teresa greatly enjoys singing with the jazz band, she can postpone the jazz performance to another semester. Taking this kind of care in accepting and scheduling solo work is essential for a student who plans on singing as a career.

Tone Quality

A choral conductor has certain expectations regarding the tone quality of an ensemble. Vowel color, vibrato, timbre, resonance, and intensity all contrib-ute to the core sound of any group of singers. The conductor's standards of tone quality can vary according to several factors, including the size of the ensemble; the collective experience or age of ensemble members; and the ensemble's repertoire.

A conductor's desired tone quality may not always be vocally comfortable for a singer. (Singers may also want to cultivate a different tone quality for themselves.) This presents a challenge: how can a singer give a conductor the tone he wants if it is not possible to produce the tone in a comfortable or healthful manner? Singers in the ensemble must do their best to match their tone to the conductor's requirements without harming their own instrument.

Certain choral literature, especially twentieth-century and new music, often requires specialized vocalizations from singers. Obviously, the astute conductor is attempting to bring about the composer's vision, and if the music calls for a specific approach, the conductor will oblige. However, singers may find some of these specialized vocalizations unwelcome. Singers wary of these techniques would be wise to stay away from ensembles that feature such literature in their repertoire.

The topic of straight-tone singing has already been discussed in chapter three. Straight-tone, or non-vibrato, singing is still the desired tone quality of some choral conductors, because of their influences, experience, and tone preferences. Singers who can produce tone without vibrato will have no problem being members of an ensemble led by such a conductor, while singers who prefer to keep vibrancy in their tone at all times will find this type of ensemble uncomfortable.

Fortunately, this absolute non-vibrato stance is diminishing among conductors as more is learned about voice science. The choral world has moved further away from the "boy-man" model and closer to a male-female countertenor gender-identified model. Modern times have created a diversity in choral singing that could not possibly have been predicted by the music masters of sixteenth-century cathedrals and churches.

Notes

1. Lloyd Pfautsch, "The Choral Conductor and the Rehearsal," in *Choral Conducting Symposium*, ed. Harold Decker and Julius Herford (Englewood Cliffs, NJ: Prentice Hall, 1988), 93.

2. Joan Dornemann, *Complete Preparation: A Guide to Auditioning for Opera* (New York: Excalibur Publishing, 1992), 26.

3. James C. McKinney, *The Diagnosis and Correction of Vocal Faults* (Nashville, TN: Genevox Music Group, 1994), 109.

4. Timothy Stalter, personal interview with the author, December 2000.

5. Into Titze, personal interview with the author, December 11, 2000.

6. Stalter, personal interview.

7. Hugh Ferguson Floyd, telephone interview with the author, November 10, 2000.

8. Stalter, personal interview.

9. Floyd, telephone interview.

10. Brenda Smith and Robert T. Sataloff, *Choral Pedagogy* (San Diego: Singular Publishing Group, 2000), 139.

11. James Luther Wrolstad, "The Effect of Choral Singing on the Developing Solo Voice" (master's thesis, California State University, Fullerton, 1979), 150.

12. Johan Sundberg, *The Science of the Singing Voice* (Dekalb: Northern Illinois University Press, 1987), 143.

13. Allen W. Goodwin, "An Acoustical Study of Individual Voices in Choral Blend," *Journal of Research in Singing and Applied Vocal Pedagogy* 13 (1989): 30.

14. Goodwin, "An Acoustical Study," 32.

15. Stalter, personal interview.

16. Paul W. Peterson, "Problems of Choral Blend," *The NATS Bulletin* 8 (1952): 2.

17. Peterson, "Problems of Choral Blend," 2.

18. Pfautsch, "The Choral Conductor and the Rehearsal," 79.

19. Ingo Titze, *Principles of Voice Production* (Englewood Cliffs, NJ: Prentice Hall, 1994), 326–27.

20. Leon Thurman and Carol Litzke, "Dealing with Vocal Distress on the Day of a Concert," *Choral Journal* 35 (1994): 31.

CHAPTER SEVEN

~

Psychological Issues
of the Choral Ensemble

Student Participation

Of all the issues facing a solo singer in a choral environment, psychological issues are among the most important. The choral conductor will want to be aware of certain realities: Why is the singer participating in choir? If the singer is a student, is choir a requirement for an academic degree? What are the professional goals of the chorus members? How much solo and choral singing experience do the members of the ensemble have? Knowing the answers to these questions will guide the conductor in his approach and help to bring out the best in his choir. In the collegiate environment students join choir for various reasons, but perhaps the most common reason is that it is required for graduation!

In his article "Treating the Choral Singer as a Person," Anthony Palmer writes:

> It has to be assumed that each person coming into a choral group comes in willingly and openly. If course requirements are being met concurrently, that is gratuity. From that, then, we must assume that each person respects the others so that the success of one is the success of all.[1]

This is an ideal sentiment, but the reality of the collegiate choral environment differs somewhat. The conductor must realize that while some vocal majors enjoy their time in choir, others may hold the opinion that it is not in their best interest as solo singers. The conductor cannot be expected to win over all the vocal majors, but he can explain the benefits of choir to them. It is imperative that the advantages of choral study be brought to the attention of vocal majors. If this is done convincingly, then neither students nor the conductor will feel their time is wasted.

Susan Sondrol Jones provides a legitimate reason why the young singer should adapt to the choral environment:

> By far, the majority of voice students who pass through voice studios in colleges and universities will be singing in ensembles as their career progresses—not having solo careers. So they need to learn how to sing correctly in an ensemble.[2]

Professor Stephen Swanson explains how involvement in the choral venue can lead to opportunities in the solo venue:

> My professional performing career was helped a great deal by choral work. I was the baritone section leader of the Chicago Symphony Orchestra for several years, and Margaret Hillis, who was the choir director at the time, used to use her section leaders to do the lead-ins until the big-time professional people came in. And in that capacity Georg Solti heard me and ended up hiring me for a small ensemble role in the Chicago Symphony Orchestra's *Moses and Aaron*.[3]

If voice faculty can convey their own positive experiences regarding choir, students may be more open to choral influences. Psychologically, the student must be in a receptive mind-set to fully benefit from the positive influences in choral singing.

Issues and Solutions

Issue: Not every voice student likes to participate in a choral ensemble.

Solution: The attitude of voice majors can improve if voice teachers and conductors make an effort to explain some benefits of choral experience to solo singers. The beginning of the semester is a great time for the conductor to speak to voice majors as a group, sharing information and answering questions. This can go a long way in bridging the gap between solo and choral singing. The benefits of choral participation are listed later in this chapter in an easy format to share with students.

Issue: To cultivate technique, a voice major must practice individually and in a manner different from the practice of choral rehearsal.

SOLUTION: Unfortunately, not everyone agrees that solo and choral singing are distinct art forms requiring distinct sets of skills. Some insist there is no significant difference between singing as a soloist and singing as a member of an ensemble. Not everyone has to agree, however, and singers can hold to their own convictions by practicing individually in a careful and consistent manner and making steady vocal progress.

ISSUE: Unlike choirs in academic settings, community and church choirs mostly contain singers without solo vocal training.

SOLUTION: Instead of requiring trained singers to modify their vibrato rates in the choral ensemble, conductors can work with less skilled singers to further develop their technique. Most conductors do not put time and effort into this endeavor, choosing instead to handpick singers with developed vibrato and vocal skills and ask them to modify or pull back their voices. Singers would be wise to speak frankly to their conducting colleagues about this issue, and to encourage them to further implement vocal training for their less experienced singers.

ISSUE: Voice teachers sometimes fail to point out the positive features of choral work.

SOLUTION: Voice teachers can use the "Benefits of Choral Participation" list later in this chapter to communicate some positive aspects of choral work to students.

ISSUE: There are more opportunities for solo singers to earn money in a choral environment than in recital, opera, or oratorio work.

SOLUTION: Expanded opportunities for choral ensemble work should be viewed in a positive light. Learning to be a competent, productive choral singer will lay the foundation for future choral work, and within the choral ensemble are opportunities for solo work. In 2007, a professional tenor at a major cathedral in Washington, DC, earned $22,000 in a part-time choral position. In East Coast metropolitan areas, a church section leader or soloist can earn a yearly salary in the $5,000 to $8,000 range for about three hours of work per week plus extra time at holidays.

The Relationship between Conductor and Ensemble

The environment of the choir is determined by the conductor's behavior and his relationship with choir members. Thomas Lloyd describes the needs of a choir in a pyramid form:

Meaning: 1. Musical emotion, symbol historical context 2. Form: pacing and structure 3. Style and sound: phrasing, articulation, balance, texture, language

4. Ear: unified pitch, rhythm, dynamics, diction and 5. Gesture: establishing and maintaining a vital pulse.[4]

The conductor's attention to each of these points will provide a structure of leadership much needed by singers.

Each musical value listed previously also applies to solo singing, but the goal and outcome of each is markedly different in choral singing. In solo singing, for example, the musical emotion must come from within individuals and their personal interpretation of the text, while in choral singing the musical emotion is indicated and directed by the conductor according to his interpretations of the music and text in rehearsal and his gestures and energy. The pacing in solo singing is a matter decided between the singer and pianist based on what the piece demands, while in choir, pacing is an issue of coordination among many people. Articulation in choral singing has to do with a group of people articulating a consonant and a rhythm with precise timing and cohesiveness, while in solo singing, articulation relates to laying emphasis on certain words for dramatic and musical effect. Unified pitch is of great importance in choral singing, but it is a nonissue in solo singing, since the individual's pitch is all that matters. Establishing and maintaining a vital pulse must be coordinated and led by the conductor in a choral setting. The vital pulse for solo singers comes from within their innermost selves.

Choral conductor Lloyd Pfautsch believes that singers must be taught to accept the musical and artistic guidance of the conductor in rehearsal and performance. He is also willing to acknowledge that conductors must realize that singers also have contributions to make in any rehearsal. Students' personal responses to the music and texts are an important part of the process. A responsive outlook from the conductor, and a spirit of active exchange between conductor and singer, are vital to the positive attitudes of students.[5]

Thomas Lloyd has explained that a kinetic connection between conductor and ensemble, particularly through gesture, can be equally important.[6] The choral conductor is in a position of power when it comes to influencing the singers in his ensemble, and his use of gesture and body expression can contribute to the ensemble's betterment or detriment. Another choral conductor gives an example:

> A common method displayed by some directors when approaching a top B♭ is to clench the fists and wave the arms violently as though to push the voices up the scale by sheer strength. As a result of these gestures the singers tighten their throats and scream with a tone that would only blend with a hog caller. In contrast to this, a practical method using good vocal taste in the same situation, would be to direct with a definite, firm, rhythmical beat to stimulate

a vitalized breath action, make some reminding gesture with the body or left hand to indicate a body "lift" or support and then relax the jaw to encourage throat freedom to allow the voice to sing in the upper register.[7]

The first portion of this quote is quite extreme, and is meant to be humorous. The second part, however, is a good illustration of a conductor's willingness to carefully consider his influence on singers through the use of his body as an expressive mechanism. Singers in such an ensemble will benefit from the conductor's thoughtfulness. Of course voice instructors can make the same kind of mistake described in the first part of the quote. Teaching in an agitated state, with extreme body tension, can also result in "screaming" and undesirable tone.

The conductor lets his leadership method be known through his use of semantics, gesture, and total body language. His gestures and attitude are of great significance to the solo singer, because they will influence the singer's technique and interpretation in choral ensemble. Some conductors may achieve positive results by creating an environment of fear and intimidation, but a calm, learning-based approach is likely to be more vocally and emotionally healthy for solo singers. A solo singer with specific concerns to discuss will benefit from opportunities to approach the conductor and communicate freely. Any discussion that leads to better understanding will improve the environment for all involved.

Just as there are different schools of singing teachers (see James McKinney's book in the bibliography), there are different schools of choral conductors. Some conductors are more ego-driven and lead their ensembles in a climate of fear and intimidation. This can be particularly unpleasant in an academic environment, where singers are not compensated for their work and are, in fact, paying for the privilege of being in the ensemble. Just as many teachers of singing are guilty of employing these methods.

The psychological dynamics of choral singing represent a significant change for the solo singer. When singing alone, the individual is the creator of vocal and emotional energy. In choir, on the other hand, energy may instead emanate from the conductor's attitude and gesturing. Patricia O'Toole refers to the discipline of the choral environment as it relates to the conductor:

Every detail of a choral rehearsal suggests discipline, from the manner in which music is taught and discussed, to the learned and highly refined gestures of the conductor. According to Michel Foucault (1979), discipline allows for the meticulous control of the operations of the body, assures the constant subjection of its forces, and imposes upon them a relationship of docility-unity. This meticulous control is achieved by controlling and defining each movement, gesture and attitude, and the rapidity by which these happen. Further, the body's movement is economized and made efficient through a constant process of persuasion.[8]

This discipline is imperative to the choral environment, as a group of singers must have a leader in order to function. However, the "meticulous control" of the conductor over the singers may not always sit well with solo singers and their teachers. We often discover in the voice studio that the letting go of discipline and control produces free and fantastic tone. Solo singers must cultivate discipline in their everyday practice, but must also release and be anti-meticulous in singing if they hope to produce an unrestrained tone. It is only when singers integrate body and mind, and develop a strong connection to the text, that exciting and meaningful dramatic interpretation can happen.

It is vital that solo singers remain aware of the conductor's influence in choir and the restoration of their own vocal energy when singing alone, without the conductor's visual clues. The dichotomy of the solo and group psychological approach must be carefully balanced by the solo singer.

The issue of the choral conductor as voice teacher cannot be ignored, as the collegiate choral conductor is in a position to exert influence regarding vocal technique perhaps more frequently than the studio teacher. The better the conductor is versed in the semantics of vocal pedagogy, the more his terminology will match that of the voice faculty. It is very useful for the solo singer to have this aural reinforcement in the choral environment.

Richard Miller states that the choral conductor should "be able to lead choristers to improved vocal proficiency."[9] He also supports the idea of pedagogical instruction during the warm-up portion of choir rehearsal:

> For every choral director, musical accuracy has to be a major priority. Training the choir to sing accurately requires time. It may seem difficult to reserve fifteen minutes of each rehearsal period to the teaching of vocal technique. Most choral conductors, however, use warm-up exercises with the choir. Improvement in intonation, attacks and releases, breath management, dynamic control, and, above all, basic choral sound, will make such an investment of time pay off handsomely. The solo singer will no longer be an alien member of the ensemble.[10]

The use and reinforcement of vocal pedagogy in the choral environment can be facilitated by open communication between choral conductor and voice faculty. The more freely pedagogical issues of choir can be discussed, the more students can maintain their vocal health and benefit from a creative learning atmosphere.

Issues and Solutions

ISSUE: The body language of the conductor may be counterproductive to easy vocal production. This is a delicate issue, but nonetheless a visual image is very powerful, and the body stance and movement of the conductor can influence choral singers.

SOLUTION: If a conductor is showing obvious tensions while conducting, singers should take care not to internalize the body and facial gesticulations of the conductor. If singers find themselves reflecting tensions of the conductor, musical interludes are a good time to release them.

ISSUE: The conductor's sense of gesture may be difficult for the singer to follow.

SOLUTION: Following a conductor is a learned skill. There are as many sets of gestures and cues as there are conductors. A clear cue is always preferable, but singers can also learn from conductors who do not give clear cues. Counting the beats of each measure should help greatly.

ISSUE: Some conductors may use fear and intimidation to control the group.

SOLUTION: Singers should seek out a conductor who respects and likes singers, even if this means participating in a less exalted group. There can be no healthy singing if singers are intimidated and fearful of a conductor. The same holds true for a singer's feelings toward a voice teacher.

ISSUE: A solo singer may be hesitant to approach a conductor to discuss vocal issues.

SOLUTION: This is a perfectly understandable fear, but many worthy conductors are happy to speak with an open mind to any singer. Choral conductors may also have a teaching assistant who is available for consultation.

ISSUE: Vocalizing may or may not be a regular part of the choral rehearsal.

SOLUTION: Singers should always do their own vocalizing before rehearsal to avoid relying on the conductor for vocal exercises. If the conductor does not include a warm-up, the solo singer is still prepared.

Benefits of Choral Participation:
What Conductors Should Tell Singers

1. *Solo opportunities are available in choir.*
   Many successful opera singers worked professionally in choral ensembles of some kind, and were able to transition from the chorus to solo status. It is possible to make this transition.
2. *Choral repertoire contains many solos for every voice type.*
   Singers who participate in chorus will have the opportunity to audition for solos. These solos are excellent opportunities for singers to work

with an orchestra, or other instrumental ensemble, and to add oratorio and other choral works to their repertoire.

3. *Singers in choir can use the experience to consider a choral career.*
Not every singer can have a solo career. There are many more opportunities to work as a professional choral singer than as a soloist. For example, the salary, benefits, and work hours of a singer in a military choir such as the U.S. Army Chorus or the Navy Sea Chanters may be comparable to solo job opportunities. Other professional choirs include the male groups Chanticleer and Cantus.

4. *Choral performance experience may lead to future job opportunities.*
Relationships with choral conductors may lead to work, and solo opportunities, with other ensembles. Conductors can provide valuable career advice to singers and help them select appropriate oratorio literature for their solo careers. The choral ensemble is an excellent place for singers to practice their professional skills.

5. *Choral rehearsal develops the skill of singing by sensation rather than sound.*
When students are presented with a less than ideal singing environment, they are forced to sing by *sensation* rather than *sound* for healthy production. It is important for the singer to learn how to sing with self-awareness of the physical mechanism. The choral experience offers the chance for singers to sing in a challenging range of performance environments.

6. *Choir is the perfect place to learn how to follow and interpret a conductor.*
Following the conductor is an essential skill for any solo singer, and choir is the ideal place to practice this skill, whether as a chorus member or a soloist within the chorus. Choir is also an opportunity to observe how other singers work with a conductor.

7. *Singing in choir develops productive and professional rehearsal behavior.*
Students in choir have an opportunity to practice professionalism that can be applied to any singing endeavor. Singers can develop professionalism by being on time, making notes in the score that are given by the conductor, respecting colleagues, using excellent technique, and arriving prepared.

8. *Choir provides an opportunity to observe how singers and instrumentalists interact.*
Students can observe firsthand the differences and dynamics between instrumentalists and singers. Singing with an instrumental ensemble is a very different experience than singing with piano. Students can also learn the role of the concertmaster or mistress, and observe how the conductor deals with orchestral issues.

9. *The art of ensemble singing can be learned through the choral experience.*
   The attitude that students take while singing in an ensemble will inform their professional work ethic. It is critical for the longevity of their careers that singers learn how to work with other singers in a group environment. This knowledge will be beneficial when they are singing in opera, small ensembles, oratorio, and many other genres.

10. *Choir offers exposure to the musical styles of major composers who also write for solo voice.*
    Composers who write choral music also write music for the solo voice. In the choral environment, singers gain exposure to these composers' musical styles and are in a better position to sing their solo compositions. For example, while singing the choral music of Benjamin Britten, singers can take notice of his method of text setting and the musical style utilized by the conductor and apply this knowledge to the singing of Britten's songs.

11. *Sight-reading skills can be greatly improved through participation in choir.*
    Improving sight-reading skills in choral rehearsal is a useful endeavor for any singer. In the real world, the faster singers can sight-read, the more jobs they can take.

12. *Choir is a rewarding and enjoyable experience.*
    Soloists may overlook the obvious: singing with a group of people can be a rewarding experience personally and musically. Choral performances bring great joy to audiences. Large choral works with orchestra reap the benefit of the well-trained voice of the soloist without imposing the soloist's performance demands.

The Solo Singer vs. Choral Singer Mind-set

We must always be careful not to make across-the-board generalizations about solo singers and choral singers and their respective mind-sets. Every singer is an individual person with diverse interests, musical and otherwise.

In the undergraduate years, vocal students are exploring many musical venues and interests. They may not classify themselves as *either* a solo or choral singer. Other vocal students are firmly committed to either solo singing or choral singing. Of course each of these endeavors should be considered a valid and worthy choice for any singer.

Sometimes vocal majors who are primarily interested in an opera career do not come to the choral ensemble with a good attitude. They may feel that chorus is not a good use of their time and not pertinent to their careers. A fundamental issue is that they are required to use their voices in a manner at odds with their solo technique. Singers who do not bring an open attitude can be detrimental to the ensemble as a whole and very unpleasant for the other singers and the conductor alike.

Solo singers would be wise to embrace the choral experience and learn whatever they can from it. Most vocal majors do not end up earning their living as solo singers. Many pursue careers outside of music, or in other branches of the performing arts. A good number of former vocal majors are pleased to find regular employment as members or section leaders of a church, community, or professional choir. The college years are a good time to explore such opportunities, speak to older, more experienced singers about career options, and learn professional behavior, all of which translate to *any* work experience, choral or solo.

Choral singers in the collegiate environment may find themselves completely at odds with the attitudes of solo singers. The performance demands and stresses of the life of a solo performer are outside the direct experience of most choral singers. These demands and stresses often foster personalities that are dramatic, emotional, outspoken, or extremely withdrawn. The choral singer practices a completely different discipline geared toward functioning as a unit, finding the group common denominator, embracing all genres of choral literature, and working with and learning from a conductor. In the collegiate environment, the choral singer who is not a vocal major is most likely a music education major or a graduate student in choral conducting or musicology. Each one of these fields is a unique discipline very different from solo singing.

In the community or church choir the singers can be divided into two groups: those who have had private study and those who have not. Some persons may identify themselves as soloists and some as choral singers. Again, judgments and absolute truths about either group must be suspended. All singers should consider themselves part of an *ensemble*, regardless of their vocal training.

In the choral ensemble, total unity of perspective and feeling is the ultimate goal. Please consider the words of a wise choral conductor:

> Singers, by themselves, cannot duplicate the exaltation or the miracle of performance which they have experienced together. And it is truly a miracle when many are led to perform with great artistry as one.[11]

Dale Moore, who champions open communication among voice professionals, writes: "I still hear from graduates . . . who look back upon their participation as long as thirty years ago in the singing of great *oratorios* as one of the most meaningful parts of their college careers. Enough said?"[12]

The ability of singers to find a balance between solo work and choral participation is of great importance during their years of matriculation. Awareness of the distinct demands of choral and solo singing will enhance their vocal study.

Tips for Singers on How to Have a Good Relationship with Your Conductor

1. Be friendly and professional to the conductor, assistant conductor, accompanist, graduate assistants, and other ensemble members.
2. Audition for every solo for which you qualify, and make sure you are perfectly prepared for the audition.
3. Come to rehearsal ready to work. Treating the experience as a professional job is excellent preparation for a solo career.
4. Commit to the process of choral rehearsal and performance and enjoy the experience.
5. For every rehearsal, be on time, seated, and ready to go before the class or rehearsal begins.
6. Bring a pencil, and when the conductor gives important instructions, actually *take notes* and refer to them when you are singing.
7. Give your best voice whenever possible, so that when you have to rest your voice, the conductor knows you are making an earnest effort.

The Relationship among Choral Conductor, Teacher of Singing, and Student

As Olaf C. Christiansen wrote in 1965, "We are all aware of the controversy among singing teachers and choral directors which has prevailed since the rebirth of choral music, back in the 1920's."[13] Each academic institution, whether a college, university, or conservatory, faces unique challenges when it comes to the relationship among choral conductors, teachers of singing, and students. Each category of individuals has its own set of viewpoints and goals, and this is how it should be. Voice students want to learn a vocal technique, have performing opportunities, and discover for themselves where their principal interests lie. The choral conductor wants to have great singers, run productive rehearsals, and develop a performing ensemble that audiences want to hear. The teacher of singing wants to teach vocal technique to her students and see them receive good performing opportunities, follow their personal goals, and achieve success. This is only a summary sketch of the goals of these individuals; the point here is that these goals are not identical.

There is an unspoken conviction in some academic environments that the teacher of singing and the choral conductor do not understand or appreciate what the other does on a daily basis. One choral conductor observes:

> There are voice teachers to whom singing in a chorus is anathema. They think choral conductors ruin voices and that there is a difference between the vocal technique used in a studio and that used in a choral rehearsal.[14]

This conductor may be right on his first point: unfortunately, there are some voice teachers who are overprotective of their students' voices and have a contentious attitude towards choral ensembles. But many other conductors and teachers, including myself, agree that the techniques used in studio and choral rehearsal *are* indeed very different. This same conductor goes on to say:

> There should be cooperative interaction and respect between private voice teachers and choral conductors, who should be working together for the same cause: assisting the development and refinement of each human instrument.
>
> . . . When there are chorus members who are studying voice privately, they should be able to recognize that the choral conductor thinks like a singer, that he is empathetic with what is involved in voice production, that he attempts to assist and to augment the vocal training received in the private studio, and that he desires to help and not inhibit the singer. The conductor's explanations, demonstrations, and vocal demands should always be consistent with what the voice student encounters in a competent private studio.[15]

Some teachers of singing feel that the choral ensemble does not best serve the solo voice, while some choral conductors feel that good solo singers should want to participate in a choral ensemble for their own benefit. Different personalities can greatly affect the interaction among faculty. As Robert Edwin writes, "Personality can include self-image, learning styles, habits, upbringing, and genetic heritage. With all these variables, probability would suggest that certain personalities will connect and others will clash."[16] For all of these reasons, choral conductors and voice teachers should not make assumptions about how the other party feels about certain issues. Acting on these assumptions can exacerbate personality conflicts.

Lack of regular interaction may aggravate the relationship between the singing teacher and choral conductor. Though both parties may be working with essentially the same group of singers, they usually do not work closely together on a regular basis. They have little opportunity to observe each other's daily routine. They may see each other only in passing, at meetings or performances. How then can they form mutual respect and a good working relationship?

It is important to remember that people who make music care passionately about what they do, and these passionate feelings carry over into their dealings with each other. Obviously they do not join the music profession for monetary reasons. A great love of music leads them to the positions they hold. These strong feelings are essential for individuals who work in the performing arts and should not be viewed negatively. At the same time, individuals' insecurities and egos should be kept in check as much as possible to form a spirit of cooperation.

It is no wonder that relations between choral conductors and teachers of singing are not always positive, given the different goals and objectives, the lack of regular interaction, and the passionate feelings. Unfortunately, in the academic environment, memories of past conflicts can linger for years and impede the progress of many.

One voice teacher uses plain words to describe scenes he has witnessed:

> In the good voice teacher-choral director relationships, the shared entities are acknowledged as such. Agreements as well as contradictions—in *fach*, technique, repertoire, and pedagogy—are talked out and through, so there can be common ground. In addition, the lines of communication are open and used as frequently as necessary. In the bad voice teacher-choral director relationships the shared entities can become the objects of a "turf war." The student singer is perceived by one or both teachers as "his" or "hers" exclusively. Like a little child grabbing at a toy and saying, "Mine!" the teacher grabs the students and says, "You're *my* student, and *I* am the final authority on your singing."[17]

This teacher makes the vital point that common ground must be actively sought to overcome differences and "send a message of cooperation to our students."[18]

This sort of comment from a choral conductor is not as helpful:

> The diva/divo attitudes that are continuously propagated by soloists frequently are more destructive to morale and group effort than all of the poor choral warm-ups that are inflicted on choirs throughout the world.[19]

This type of generalization should be avoided by all parties involved if communication and understanding are to move to the next level. No doubt such bad attitudes exist among soloists, but antagonistic language like "continuously propagated" does not indicate a collegiate openness on the part of this conductor.

Other choral conductors speak of a spirit of unity among faculty and students. Singers and conductors work together on many aspects of music making: producing pure vowels, sustained *legato* style, articulation, declamatory style, controlled dynamics, expanding pitch and color range, flexibility, musicianship, and listening habits.[20] Most voice teachers and conductors would have to agree that these aspects of music making are relevant to both solo and choral singers.

Choral conductor Louis H. Diercks, describing his attention to the solo singer in his ensembles over a 35-year career, writes that he "endeavored to successfully develop choral tone without interrupting or undoing the work of the private voice teacher."[21] Voice teachers and singers should be aware that many choral conductors today share his view. Relations among all parties do not have to be contentious, but for everyone to function in a healthy manner, attitudes need to improve and communication needs to increase.

How Choral Conductors and Teachers of Singing Can Coexist

1. The parties have to acknowledge that choral singing is a distinct art form from solo singing, requiring different skills and standards.
2. The parties have to agree that there is great value in what the other does.
3. The parties have to agree that choral and solo singing do not always require the same type of singer.
4. The parties have to acknowledge that some solo singers are not choral singers and some choral singers are not solo singers.
5. The parties have to accept the fact that modification of solo technique is absolutely necessary in a choral ensemble.
6. The singing teacher has to accept that the choral conductor believes soloists can sing in a healthy manner in a choral ensemble.
7. The choral conductor has to accept that the voice teacher might not see modification of technique as vocally healthy for a singer.
8. Both parties need to observe each other in the teaching environment.
9. Both parties need to attend performances that represent each other's work.
10. Both parties need to maintain flexibility when it comes to working with a singer.
11. Both parties need to speak openly and without rancor when conflicting opinions arise.

12. When communicating with a student, both parties need to speak about each other with professionalism and respect. Better yet, if a student has an issue in choir, the three parties should speak together.
13. Finally, choral and vocal faculty have to work together with administrators in the recruiting and hiring of new music faculty who will work with and influence singers.

Paul W. Peterson offers a parting thought on this crucial topic: "Sensitivity to beauty coupled with proper vocal techniques will close the barrier between choir directors and voice teachers who are engaged in a common goal of inspiring our youth to higher vocal standards in a singing America."[22]

What Singers Want from Choral Conductors
1. The opportunity to use their complete voice, without undue modification, in the choral ensemble.
2. Proper classification in a choral part and the flexibility to switch parts if there are changes in the voice.
3. No expectation of a singer to compensate vocally for another singer with less vocal ability or willingness to sing.
4. Superior choral literature that is conducive to good singing.
5. Lenience when singers are sick, vocally fatigued, or otherwise unable to sing.
6. The conductor's trust that the singer will sing in choral rehearsal whenever possible.
7. Realistic vocal demands during choral rehearsal.
8. An environment that is professional and collegial.
9. Fair consideration when auditioning for choral solos.
10. Any career advice a conductor may find relevant for a particular singer.

Notes

1. Anthony J. Palmer, "Treating the Choral Singer as a Person," *Choral Journal* 22 (1981): 31.

2. Susan Sondrol Jones, personal interview with the author, November, 2000.

3. Stephen Swanson, personal interview with the author, November, 2000.

4. Thomas Lloyd, "Am I Being Followed? Finding the Elusive Connection between Conductor and Ensemble," *Choral Journal* 36 (1996): 24.

5. Lloyd Pfautsch, "The Choral Conductor and the Rehearsal," in *Choral Conducting Symposium*, ed. Harold A. Decker and Julius Herford (Englewood Cliffs, NJ: Prentice Hall, 1988), 94.

6. Lloyd, "Am I Being Followed?" 25.

7. Paul W. Peterson, "Problems of Choral Blend," *The NATS Bulletin* 8 (1952): 2.

8. Patricia O'Toole, "I Sing in a Choir But I Have No Voice!" *The Quarterly Journal of Music Teaching and Learning* (Winter–Spring 1993): 65–76.

9. Richard Miller, *On the Art of Singing* (New York: Oxford University Press, 1996), 58–59.

10. Miller, *On the Art of Singing*, 63.

11. Peterson, "Problems of Choral Blend," 2.

12. Dale Moore, "A Plea for Dialogue," *The NATS Journal* (January–February 1990): 3.

13. Olaf C. Christiansen, "Solo and Ensemble Singing," *The NATS Bulletin* (February 1965): 16.

14. Pfautsch, "The Choral Conductor and the Rehearsal," 93.

15. Pfautsch, "The Choral Conductor and the Rehearsal," 93, 98.

16. Robert Edwin, "The Good, the Bad, and the Ugly: Singing Teacher–Choral Director Relationships," *Journal of Singing* (May–June 2001): 53.

17. Edwin, "The Good, the Bad, and the Ugly," 53.

18. Edwin, "The Good, the Bad, and the Ugly," 53.

19. The conductor is Edward Byrom, quoted in Ingo Titze, "Edward Byrom's Reply to 'Choir Warm-Ups: How Effective Are They?'" *Journal of Singing* 58 (September–October 2001): 57.

20. For example, see Peterson, "Problems of Choral Blend," 2.

21. Louis H. Diercks and E. Milton Boone, "The Individual in the Choral Situation," *The NATS Bulletin* 17 (May 1961): 6.

22. Peterson, "Problems of Choral Blend," 2.

CHAPTER EIGHT

~

Interpretive Issues
of the Choral Ensemble

Interpreting Emotion through the Voice

Dramatic interpretation is an essential issue for the solo singer. In colleges and universities, vocal majors learn to integrate the interpretation of emotions and drama into their performance technique. Acting classes and opera workshops often provide an environment in which to explore these skills. In the choral environment, interpreting emotion through the voice as an ensemble is a complex issue. How can a group of people express the same emotion at the exact same time? The choir may create a general mood—or a very specific one, depending on the conductor and choir in question—while the solo singer is individually responsible for creating a *specific* dramatic intent each moment while singing.

Walter Foster explains how imagination is a central element of singing:

> The imaginative capacity is central to the singing event in all respects. The awakening, development, and participation of the singer's imagination constitutes an integral part of a meaningful pedagogy, because it is the imaginative capacity that (1) makes possible the conceptualization for the singing tone in all its aspects, and (2) directly kindles the emotional process that energizes, initiates, and coordinates the singing response.[1]

In other words, the emotional intent of the singer is strongly integrated into the vocal production. If solo singers participating in choir do not have a specific emotional intent, their vocal energy may be lessened, and they may not help the group communicate to its audience.

Many choral conductors are well aware of the importance of emotional connection to music. As John Dickson states, "The singer must absorb the words into his or her own experience or he or she remains void of any real existence. Conductors must make every effort to connect the singers' experience with the words they are singing."[2]

A more detailed method of analyzing text, used by solo singers, is the *monologue technique*, described here by Lyn Schenbeck:

> Musical theater coach Fred Silver describes a monologue technique that can guide singers through a text. The first step is to analyze the lyric by creating a summary of what is being said. Step two is to find the essential, nonessential, color, and descriptive words. The third step is to experience the emotion of the text. In the case of phenomena with which the singer cannot identify, they can try to remember something real that has made them feel similarly, even if it is unrelated to the actual song. Actors call this device emotional substitution. Step four is to integrate knowledge of the text with the singer's own personality. The final part of the process is to reintegrate everything learned about the text with its realization in musical elements such as phrasing, pauses and dynamics.[3]

The monologue technique might be interesting for members of the choir and the conductor to explore. Any time the conductor spends on text interpretation will benefit the performance of the choir. Text interpretation is best done early in the learning process so that music and text will be completely integrated. As Schenbeck writes, "Rehearsal time can be well invested in presenting a text to a choir early in the rehearsal process—before their first read through of the music—to enhance their understanding of the entire piece."[4]

The solo singer will greatly appreciate any effort the conductor makes to bring textual interpretation to the attention of the choir. Solo singers can also offer to share their knowledge about interpretation in general with other members of the group.

Example of Monologue Technique

The text for this example is from J. S. Bach's *St. Matthew Passion, BWV 224*: "The world, with treachery replete, with lies and fraud and false deceit would tangle and ensnare me. Lord, keep Thou me from danger free, from evil malice spare me!"

1. Create a summary of what is being said:

   "God, the world is dangerous, please keep me safe!"

2. Find essential, nonessential, color, and descriptive words:

   Essential words: world, Lord, me

   Nonessential words: the, with, and, would, from

   Color/descriptive words: treachery, lies, fraud, false deceit, tangle, ensnare, danger, evil, malice

3. Experience the emotion of the text:

   Ask yourself: "When have I prayed? When have I asked someone for help? What emotions do I experience when I feel threatened? What is dangerous in the world, to me? What has happened to make me feel afraid?" Also try the technique of emotional substitution, applying an emotional memory that rouses compatible emotions. Think of a time in your life when you have prayed for help and been genuinely afraid, or when you have experienced evil in a personal way.

4. Integrate knowledge of the text with your own personality:

   Ask yourself: "How can my personal experiences and feelings help me relate to this text?"

5. Integrate text with musical elements:

   After internalizing the text, take a look at the music. How do the composer's musical choices help to emphasize the emotions of the words? How can you make the most of these elements to further express your interpretation?

Issues and Solutions

ISSUE: Some choral conductors may not focus on the emotional life behind the text during regular choral rehearsal.

SOLUTION: Conductors should consider including text study in the daily rehearsal. The five minutes immediately after the warm-up may be a good time for the conductor to isolate one or two phrases and encourage discussion among the choir. Asking questions of choir members is a productive way to stimulate discussion: What do you think is the essential meaning of this text? To whom do you think this character is singing? What words in this phrase are significant?

SOLUTION: Another idea for improving interpretive skills is to devote time during sectional rehearsals for discussing textual meaning. If choir members have the opportunity to examine the text, they will find ways to relate to it personally and may feel more passionately about the music.

SOLUTION: A third suggestion is to assign specific texts at the beginning of the semester to various students in the choir. They are then responsible for analyzing the text and sharing the results with the choir. When students personalize the text, instead of depending on the conductor to convey ideas, they will involve themselves more fully in the interpretive process.

ISSUE: The dramatic presentation by the choral ensemble may be too *general* in mood. Specificity is essential for a meaningful and interesting performance.

SOLUTION: Working individually and collectively, choral conductors and singers can make every attempt to connect personally to the text and apply specific emotional intent during performance.

Integrated Music/Drama Performance

Choral conductors may not be able to devote much time to the interpretation of text during the choral rehearsal. Coordination of pitch and rhythm may instead be the primary focus. In the private studio, the singer and teacher often spend time discussing the meaning and emotional interpretation of text. But in choir, students may have to modify, if not altogether eliminate, their interpretive ideas to fit within the style of the group and not draw attention to themselves. Because the conductor is the leader and must determine his own textual interpretation, singers cannot individually interpret text in the choral environment. When a conductor communicates his desire for emotional intent in the interpretation of choral music, solo singers respond and invest more of their emotional selves in the music.

Today, more than ever, solo singers are expected to present a specific dramatic interpretation in their singing performance. The old days of "stand and sing" are no longer acceptable to most audience members, unless a singer is in possession of a truly powerhouse voice. The international audience expects drama with their singing!

Singers achieve this drama through much practice, and dramatic studies are a vital component of the curriculum for conservatory voice students. Voice teachers are constantly looking for ways to inspire and teach their students to connect emotionally with the text. Aspiring opera singers seek out drama, acting, and improvisation classes to augment their scene study and aria classes.

Why is dramatic interpretation not a regular component of most choral ensemble rehearsals and performance? Is there simply too much to accomplish in regard to unifying the musical elements, so that attention to the text is postponed? On a deeper level, what exactly is the choral ensemble's performance goal when it comes to interpreting the text? It cannot be denied that choral music is text-based, like solo voice music.

The reality is that the dramatic element is sometimes absent in choral performance, even when an influx of drama would greatly raise the excitement level. The issue then becomes: How can a group of people express a united emotion? Is this a chimerical goal? These ideas are certainly worth exploring in the choral environment, with the active involvement of the choral conductor.

A *Choral Journal* article asks, "Rehearsal time is precious: how can a director efficiently convey the background of a text in any detail and depth?"[5] A text written by a singer and choral conductor offers suggestions to conductors on how to better integrate textual meaning into the rehearsal. These suggestions range from the solemn to the humorous; here is one of the humorous examples:

> To increase a feeling for the body and to activate the breathing muscles, follow with hopping, skipping, and humming. Then smell a wonderful bouquet of fragrant spring flowers, or taste a ripe peach which makes the mouth water.[6]

This suggestion is steeped in imagery but may work for some choirs. Solo singers might undertake a similar exercise in an improvisation or acting class. Solo singers might respond to the fragrant spring flowers and ripe peaches, or they may not. In any case, suggested exercises such as this one are surprisingly scarce in the literature. More suggestions are needed from conductors and voice teachers alike.

The composers of choral literature were inspired by specific texts and wrote music to animate them. Choral conductors and singers are capable of giving choral texts the attention they deserve, and this attention will benefit performers and audience alike.

Issues and Solutions

ISSUE: In the choral environment, the conductor may not spend time on dramatic aspects of performance.

SOLUTION: Solo singers should take responsibility for preparing their choral texts in the same manner as their solo texts. Analyzing choral texts is excellent practice for solo work. During choir rehearsal, there should also be ample time to analyze the text while other sections are rehearsing. Singers who invest time interpreting the text will connect to the music more easily and approach performance with a greater personal investment.

The Relevance of Choral Texts

Solo singers in choral ensembles would be wise to pay close attention to the texts they sing in rehearsal and performance. There is a strong possibility that these same texts and poets will show up in their solo repertoire! The texts of choral pieces by Ralph Vaughan Williams and Benjamin Britten, for example, also appear in these composers' solo literature.

Composers of choral music and solo literature also adapt many of the same poets. Singers can learn the literary style and themes of these poets in choir, and then apply that knowledge to their solo repertoire. For example, singing choral texts of German composers such as Felix Mendelssohn and Robert Schumann can prepare the solo singer for the symbolism employed by German poets. Singing the choral texts of J. S. Bach can prepare the solo singer to handle repeated text with emotional intent and variation—a skill that can then be applied to Bach arias. Folk texts in Benjamin Britten's choral pieces also show up in arrangements for the solo singer.

If solo singers are wise, they will use their time in choir to learn as much as possible about the poetry of choral music. The obvious, but critically important, point to be made about choral texts is that they exist! Choral music is ultimately an expression of words and thoughts, just like solo vocal music. Singers and conductors should never approach any vocal music without consideration of the applicable text. The emotional and dramatic thrust of the text informed the composer and continues to inform the music itself.

How to Analyze a Choral Poetic Text

Many methods can be applied for analyzing text for performance; Fred Silver's monologue technique was explained earlier in this chapter. Any credible acting textbook will include methods of analyzing text, as will many books on opera performance and poetic interpretation.

During choral rehearsals, the solo singer will most likely have plenty of time to closely examine the applicable text while the conductor works with individual sections. These study opportunities deepen the singer's intellectual and emotional connection to the text in choir, and also serve as practice for analyzing texts in solo literature. Here is a simple plan for analysis:

1. Write out the complete text on a piece of paper. You do not need to repeat lines of text that are repeated in the score. Looking at the words apart from their musical structure is key.

2. After reading over the text carefully, write one sentence that conveys the meaning of the poem. (Examples could include "The beauty of nature brings great joy to all people," "Even though you bring me nothing but sorrow I love you," or "Drinking and dancing is fun.")

3. Become a character by adopting a perspective or attitude conveyed by the poet. Write down how your character thinks; for example, "I am seeking love," "I am expressing anger toward the authority," or "I am praising God for his many blessings."

4. From this perspective or attitude, formulate an overall objective, beginning with the words "I want to . . ."; for example, "I want to find love," "I want to destroy my enemy," or "I want to entertain people." Write this objective at the top of the piece of paper.

5. Working with your objective and the musical score, choose an emotion word for each line of text and write it at the end of the line ("angry," "thrilled," "stunned," "depressed"). Use the musical feeling of each line to influence your choice. The more active and specific the emotion, the better. Avoid less specific words such as "sad" and "happy."

6. Write these emotion words above the lines of text in the score. If the text repeats, use the same emotion word.

7. Divide the score into sections according to the musical language. (One piece might have three sections, while another may have six or seven.) Where does the music change? Rhythm, tempi, and dynamic shifts can all indicate a change in mood, as can textual elements.

8. Look at the emotion words within each section. Pick the word that best expresses all the emotion words, and write it at the beginning of the section. This word will be your *focus emotion* as you sing that section; you will infuse the text with the emotion of the word you have chosen.

9. After all these steps are completed, focus on integrating the overall objective with the emotion words. Take note of the emotional transitions from one section to another, and the ways in which these emotional transitions are marked by musical transitions. If this entire technique is conscientiously applied, the singer will never sing choral music on "automatic pilot," but with real emotion and meaning.

Example of Analysis of a Choral Text

1. From G. F. Handel's *Messiah*: "And the glory of the Lord shall be revealed, and all flesh shall see it together, for the mouth of the Lord hath spoken it."

2. Everyone will see the miracles of God.
3. "I am announcing the miracles of God."
4. "I want to give hope."
5. "And the glory of the Lord shall be revealed"—*thrilled.*
   "And all flesh shall see it together"—*excited.*
   "For the mouth of the Lord hath spoken it"—*reverent.*
6. *thrilled, thrilled, excited, excited, excited, excited, thrilled, reverent, reverent, reverent, reverent.*
7. Sections one, two and three, corresponding to the three lines of text.
8. Section one—*thrilled.*
   Section two—*excited.*
   Section three—*reverent.*
9. Continually find freshness and relevance in the text when it is repeated.

How to Analyze a Foreign Language Choral Text

Singing in a foreign language is a challenge for any singer, whether the genre is solo or choral literature. If a singer is fluent in a foreign language, interpretation is obviously much easier. But pronunciation and translation are only the first steps in connecting to a foreign text. After the International Phonetic Alphabet (IPA) conversion and word-for-word translation are completed, the singer is ready to analyze the foreign text, as follows:

1. Write the complete IPA transliteration beneath the foreign language text in the score. If the text repeats, repeating the translation is optional.
2. Chose either a literal word-for-word or poetic English translation to write above the foreign text in the score. (If English is not your first language, use your own language here.) Which type of translation you choose is up to you. If there is already an acceptable translation in the score, it is perfectly fine to use that. If you suspect the translation is second-rate, use available sources to find a better one. One hint: if there are many rhyming words, the translation is probably not very good!
3. Once you can pronounce the words and have a good translation written in the score, it is time to create the *subtext*—that is, the text that lies figuratively beneath the words of the poem and infuses the text with emotion. The subtext is what your character is *really* saying when you sing the foreign words.
4. Using the English translation, go through the score and beneath each line write subtext that reflects your gut interpretation of the text. For

example, if a line of translation reads "When I go to the garden, your spirit is in the flowers and trees," your subtext might be "When I go to the garden, I feel you there in everything." Or if the line reads "Off to battle to fight the sworn enemy!" your subtext could be "I fight the ones I hate!" Freedom of choice and personal feelings will color your subtext. Feel free to use strong language and words that you use in everyday life. The point is to give the text a sense of immediacy.

5. After the subtext is completed, choose an overall objective (as in step 4 of the previous exercise) and write it on the first page of the score. For each line of subtext, choose an emotion word that fits (as in step 5 of the previous exercise). You do not have to think of a different emotion word for every single line. Be sure to let the musical language of the piece help you decide whether to change emotions from line to line.

6. Divide the score into sections (as in step 7 of the previous exercise) and assign one emotion word to each section. The emotion words should be contrasting and very active.

7. Practice reading the subtext aloud while feeling the emotion you have chosen. Remember to observe the contrasts and changes in musical and emotional mood.

8. While rehearsing and singing the foreign text, think the subtext, or read it, since you will most likely have the score in front of you. When you are comfortable with thinking the subtext, start adding the emotional component. Now *feel* the emotion, *think* the subtext, and *sing* the foreign language text at once. This process will continue for as long as you work on the piece. This is the same method used by solo singers. You have an advantage in the choral setting, since the music is not usually memorized, and while singing you can *read* the subtext and emotion words written in the score. After you have trained your mind to focus in this way, try applying this same technique to solo repertoire. Is it now easier to connect with the text dramatically?

The Physical Self in Choral Performance

In solo singing, the realm of dramatic interpretation is closely tied to the physical self. Because singers carry their instruments inside their bodies, they must use their bodies as a means of expression.

In choral singing, the soloist may have to subdue the body as well as the voice. To remain part of the group, singers in the choral ensemble must keep their bodies more or less still. Expressing music through physical movement during performance might be distracting to audience members, other singers, and the conductor. Some choir members do move about in a conspicuous manner during performance, but they tend to look ridiculous and inauthentic in a group setting. Singers who strive for an overall energized body are much better off than those singers who move their body in a false or forced manner.

Some solo singers' techniques are strongly tied into their physical selves, and physical modification may be difficult for them to sustain throughout choral performance. It is therefore critical that singers release tensions before, during, and after choral performance with the exercises suggested in this book. Singers can also focus on the inner emotional approach to the music rather than the outward approach.

Notes

1. Walter C. Foster, *Singing Redefined: A Conceptual Approach to Singing* (Huntsville, TX: Recital Publications, 1998), 24.

2. John Dickson, "Musical Pride and Textual Prejudice: The Expressivity of Language in Choral Music," *Choral Journal* 36 (1993): 11.

3. Lyn Schenbeck, "Finding the Poet's Voice: Strategies for Collective Interpretation of Choral Text," *Choral Journal* 40 (2000): 13.

4. Schenbeck, "Finding the Poet's Voice," 14.

5. Schenbeck, "Finding the Poet's Voice," 13.

6. Wilhelm Ehmann and Frauke Haasemann, *Voice Building for Choirs* (Englewood Cliffs, NJ: Prentice Hall, 1988), 22.

CHAPTER NINE

~

Acoustic Issues
of the Choral Ensemble

In the choral environment several voices are singing together, so the acoustic load is much larger and more complex than in solo singing. How much a singer listens to others while singing in choir depends on the individual. However, there can be no doubt that the sound of other voices can affect an individual's vocal production.[1]

Ingo Titze explains how the choral environment makes it difficult to monitor one's own vocal production:

> It's hard to determine how to balance your loudness (intensity) with someone standing right next to you. You're getting your own sound from the side, you don't know what sound is going straight from your mouth. And so you have to balance your loudness to persons on either side of you based on what you hear laterally. Sometimes what you get from one ear is different from what you get from the other ear, and the quality is different and the vowels are different. . . . The whole idea of loudness and pitch is greatly affected by whether you make your vowels the same.[2]

Scientific evidence has demonstrated that in a group setting, individual singers cannot accurately perceive or measure other voices in themselves or in relation to their own voices. A study of choral singing conducted by Sten Ternström and Johan Sundberg notes the sound pressure levels in choir:

> Here we may mention that the sound the singers heard from the rest of the choir varies around the 80dB [decibel] sound pressure level, according to measurements

made in two choirs. However, considerable higher values also occur; in a soprano section, a 115dB sound pressure level occurred several times.[3]

The study goes on to explain how the 80dB level is not harmful to the singer, because of the ear's ability to protect itself: "Such loud sounds would not be detrimental to hearing, because the sensitivity of the hearing organ is decreased as soon as one starts to phonate; a muscle in the middle ear reflexively contracts so that the level reaching the inner ear is reduced."[4]

Before discussing how singers perceive each other's voices, we should first understand how we hear our own voices. Sundberg writes many factors are at work in the self-perception of sound:

> To summarize, how we perceive our own voice depends on four different factors: (1) the frequency dependent ability of sound to travel backwards from the lip opening to the ears, (2) the frequency dependent ability of the walls, floor and ceiling of the room to reflect sound, i.e., the room acoustics, (3) the frequency dependent ability of the sound in the vocal tract to transform into vibrations in the vocal tract wall structures, and (4) the frequency dependent ability of the bone structure of the skull to transmit vibrations from the vocal tract walls to the inner ear. From these four points it is quite evident that the timbre of one's own voice is dependent upon the room acoustics, among other things, and this makes the auditory feedback a whimsy judge of the quality of one's own phonation.[5]

Based on the above data, it is safe to conclude that singers are at an acoustical disadvantage when it comes to hearing themselves, and cannot hear themselves as others hear them. The shape and size of a room and the structure of a singer's anatomy are just two factors relating to acoustic function that are beyond the control of the individual singer. This is precisely why the ability to sing by sensation is so vital for the solo singer in the choral setting. The ability to perceive one's own voice by sensation rather than sound is a fundamental tool of a singer's vocal technique and can be cultivated while participating in choir.

As Allen Goodwin writes, the singer's need to match the output of other choir members can result in acoustic modification:

> It is a common observation that singers attempting to blend reduce their dynamic level to avoid being conspicuously loud in the ensemble. The results of this study suggest that choral singers may adjust their overall intensity not only to affect the perceived loudness of their tones, but also to create other acoustical changes in their vocal sounds, which the singers perceive as helpful

for achieving vocal blend. . . . Reducing the overall intensity also has shown to produce complementary changes in vowel quality and vocal registration, particularly when detrimental qualities are associated with over-singing.[6]

The singer's desire to achieve "vocal blend" can be strong in the choral setting, creating potential difficulties when the singer returns to solo singing. Any vocal modification or lessening of intensity must be reversed in order to produce the vocal energy needed for solo singing.

Issues and Solutions

ISSUE: Conductors encourage choral singers to listen to one another.

SOLUTION: Singers should take such encouragement with a grain of salt, as Ternström and Sundberg have scientifically demonstrated that other voices are impossible to discern objectively in the choral environment.

ISSUE: The sound of other voices can affect individual vocal production.

SOLUTION: Singers can learn to focus on the abdominal and facial sensations of singing instead of self-auditory feedback. To avoid excessive interference from other voices, avoid standing in front of singers with loud voices. Standing in the back row or at the end of a row is ideal.

ISSUE: Choral singers feel an often unconscious need to match the vocal output of other singers in the group. This can result in oversinging.

SOLUTION: Solo singers must monitor their voices after choir for any signs of extreme fatigue. Is their speaking voice hoarse? Do they have any difficulty phonating sounds? If the answer to either of these questions is yes, they are most likely oversinging in the ensemble. Voice production should remain as close as possible to the technique used in solo singing. Singing by sensation and self-monitoring are the best ways to preserve the voice.

ISSUE: Singers make acoustical changes in their vocal output if they perceive the need to blend. Repetitive or prolonged modification of the vocal technique may be damaging to the solo singer over time, and can result in incorrect muscle memory. For example, if solo singers in choir feel the need to pull back their intensity and vibrato on a high and soft pitch, they may end up applying this same technique as a soloist. A pitch that is soft, blended, and vibrato-free in the choral context may come across in the solo context as no-resonance, unsupported, and uninteresting.

SOLUTION: Singers can engage in warm-down *vocalises* after choral rehearsal. Regular vocalizing sessions will help the solo singer balance modifications made in choral rehearsal.

Teaching Example

William, a *basso-profondo*, is a senior vocal major at a Big Ten university. He is 23 years old and in possession of a large-sized, resonant, and powerful instrument. He is planning to pursue opera as a career. He participates in an elite ensemble at school with only six singers on each voice part. After a recent choral performance, he heard comments from several people that his voice was the only bass voice heard for the entire concert. Someone even told him that she could hear his voice over the entire choir throughout the concert. William thinks this is very good news.

William is not unusual in his opinion. He has the mind-set of a soloist and feels that being heard is always a positive! This student is not suited for the choral environment, but is required to participate while in school. His teacher should probably speak with him about some of the differences between solo and choral singing. The teacher can suggest to William that he lessen his vocal intensity in choir, so that other singers may be heard. Throughout rehearsals and performances, William should check to make sure he can perceive other voices; if not, he is probably singing too loudly.

William is an example of the solo singer who refuses to make adjustments or modifications to his technique when in the choral environment. In the best-case scenario, the conductor of the ensemble would take care of this issue early in the academic year by speaking to the singer one-on-one.

Feedback and Reference

Knowledge of *feedback* and *reference* sounds will promote the singer's vocal health while participating in a choral ensemble. Sten Ternström defines "feedback" as the sound of one's own voice, while "reference" refers to the sound of the rest of the choir.[7] As he states, "The level difference between the feedback and the reference is one of the more important acoustic factors in choir singing."[8]

The reference sound and feedback sound are equally affected by the physical dimensions of the room, but the reference sound has unique dynamics. Reflecting surfaces, proximity of other singers, and the absorption area of the room will all influence reference sounds.

Ternström explains that the conductor can do several things to decrease the volume of the reference sounds and thereby more accurately imitate the solo singer's environment:

> If the reference is so loud that the singers find it hard to hear their own voices, they could be assisted by increasing the room absorption or by increasing the

spacing between singers. . . . It helps to mix the sections of the choir so that section colleagues are not standing next to each other. A singer's section colleagues sing the same notes and the same text, and are therefore the most efficient maskers of his or her feedback.[9]

Electrical engineer E. Milton Boone has also demonstrated that singers not surrounded by others in their section can more accurately evaluate their own voices in terms of intonation, dynamics, tone color, and diction.[10] The technique of breaking up sections of singers has been used by many notable conductors over the years, including Robert Shaw.[11]

As these professionals have confirmed, the spacing and positioning of choir members is crucial. Ternström adds that inserting one's finger into the ear can help shut out reference sounds. He also suggests using a music binder to deflect airborne feedback of other choir members.[12] Of course placing the finger on the ear or holding a music binder to the head—however helpful to the singer in rehearsal—would be distracting to the audience in performance.

Issues and Solutions

ISSUE: Every singer in choir will hear a multitude of "reference" sounds when singing.

SOLUTION: Singers need to create as much space around themselves as possible in order to mask reference sounds. Conductors need to space out the singers so that reference sounds are reduced.

SOLUTION: In rehearsal, a finger placed on the ear or a binder held over the ear may reduce reference sounds. These tactics may distract or even offend other singers, but they do work.

ISSUE: Singers from the same section are most likely to mask each other's sounds since they sing the same vowels and pitches.

SOLUTION: Conductors can mix the singers so that they are not singing next to members of their section. Soprano could stand next to alto, tenor next to bass, and so on. This arrangement will also minimize reference sounds.

Teaching Example

Daniel, a tenor, is 45 years old and a member of a prestigious community choir in the Mid-Atlantic region. He never studied voice formally, yet has a solid technique and a lovely instrument. He has sung in professional choirs most of his adult life and enjoys it very much. He is a new member to this particular choir. Recently he has noticed that his tuning seems off during rehearsal and that he has trouble finding his starting pitches for the Tenor II part. In addition, after rehearsal, his speaking voice is very tired and slightly hoarse. None of these problems have plagued him in the past.

Daniel felt so shaky in the last performance that he has started to lose confidence in his abilities as a choir member. He is confused and frustrated and is seeking a voice teacher to help him with his issues.

Daniel does not have any sense of feedback for his own voice in choir. His voice is completely masked by the reference sounds of the very loud bass singers standing directly behind him in rehearsal and performance. In the choir's semicircular formation, basses surround Daniel on three sides. Because of their reference sounds, Daniel is having tuning problems and cannot find his starting pitches. He is also oversinging in a futile effort to increase his feedback.

Daniel may be disoriented by the singer formation in the new ensemble as well as the lack of feedback. He might try changing places or moving to the end of a row.

The Lombard Effect

The solo singer who participates regularly in choir should be aware of the *Lombard effect,* an acoustic event described by Steven Tonkinson as follows:

> There is masking of an individual voice by the sound of surrounding voices. This masking effect leaves the individual choral singer with less than a desired amount of auditory feedback. I have observed that when the masking effect occurs in the choral environment, there is a tendency for singers to push or force their voices to enhance feedback. This tendency is known as the "Lombard Effect."[13]

This choral phenomenon may pose some risk to the solo singer. Any subconscious pushing or forcing of the voice for an extended time can cause fatigue or long-term damage to the voice. Every choral singer is at risk for the Lombard effect regardless of voice type or age. Tonkinson's study concludes that "most of the choral singers in this study, regardless of experience, tended to succumb to a Lombard effect when faced with increasing loss of auditory feedback."[14]

The young singer is particularly susceptible to the Lombard effect in choir. While singing in choir, solo singers must continually check their own vocal output and resist the urge to increase the volume for better hearing and feedback. Fatigue following a choral rehearsal could be a symptom of the Lombard effect.

Issues and Solutions

Issue: The young, inexperienced singer is susceptible to the Lombard effect in the choral environment. This pushing of the voice to enhance one's own feedback can bring about vocal fatigue and even cause damage if practiced for prolonged periods of time.

Solution: The solo singer should be aware that the Lombard effect is a common hazard of choral singing, and that vocal awareness is the best defense. If excess fatigue and loss of voice occur on a regular basis after choral rehearsals, the student may be experiencing symptoms of the Lombard effect.

Teaching Example

Sally, a mezzo-soprano, is a sophomore vocal major. She is working on mezzo-soprano solo literature and participates in a choral ensemble four days a week. Each choral rehearsal lasts about ninety minutes, with one ten-minute break. At lessons, as she is vocalizing, her teacher notices some raspiness in the sound, especially through the second *passaggio*, as well as a tiny delay in phonation on an exercise of *staccato* arpeggios. When the teacher questions Sally, she responds that she is "vocally tired" and not sure why. This same scenario occurs several weeks in a row. At the conclusion of each lesson, the teacher notices that Sally's speaking voice is hoarse.

Sally's ensemble is made up of music majors and non-majors. Not all of the singers in the ensemble read music well or have had vocal training. As a voice major in the alto section, Sally is the *de facto* section leader as the other singers look to her for vocal leadership. In fact, many altos wait for her to start each phrase before they sing. Sally feels a responsibility to "carry" the section vocally, as the conductor has recognized her as a leader on several occasions.

A delay at the start of phonation is a warning sign for a singer. The hoarseness in Sally's speaking voice, the raspiness in her sung tone, and the delay in phonation are all indicators of vocal trauma. Sally is probably oversinging in the choral environment, and, in combination with her other singing obligations, has damaged her voice. A ninety-minute rehearsal is extremely long for someone singing loudly most of the time. Including her individual practice, she is probably singing twice as much as she should each weekday.

Students who exhibit hoarseness in the speaking voice (and do not have a cold or infection) for more than two lessons should visit the laryngologist to have their vocal folds visualized.

Sally's oversinging is probably caused by a combination of issues. The acoustic load of other singers is distorting her own feedback, so she is experiencing the Lombard effect, unconsciously singing louder to increase her feedback. She is also trying to compensate for the deficiencies of other singers in the section who are not meeting the conductor's expectations. Sally has disregarded her vocal health and has overextended her voice.

Sally should go on vocal rest until she is seen by the doctor. If there is no visable damage to the vocal fold nodules, she should ask the doctor when she can start singing again. If there is damage, she will have to follow the doctor's regimen, which will most likely include medication, voice therapy, rest, and follow-up visits.

Sally will need to learn how not to compensate for other singers in the choral setting. It is her responsibility not to let their behavior dictate her behavior. She might try switching seats in rehearsal on a regular basis. She should also monitor her vocal output throughout the rehearsal to make sure she is singing healthfully. In the future, she would probably benefit by resting her voice completely at least two days a week. She could also use a marking technique in choral rehearsal part of the time, assuming she can do it well.

Sally's situation is a common example of how other singers can affect an individual's voice in the choral setting. Occasionally in the academic choral setting, vocal majors will leave the "heavy lifting" to another singer in an effort to preserve their own voice, or out of plain laziness. It is a grave mistake to try to cover up for these individuals by singing louder, harder, or longer. One voice is one voice only; it cannot make an entire section.

The Singers' Formant in the Choral Ensemble

The *singers' formant* is the ring, or peak of acoustic energy, in the 2000–3000Hz range of the voice. The singers' formant is what allows the human voice to carry over the piano and instrumental ensembles.

Research has suggested that choral singers do not utilize the singers' formant, and this widely published finding has perhaps influenced many singers in preparing for their ensemble work.[15] Recent scientific research presents an even more complicated picture. In a study by Rossing and others, the tones of male and female singers were compared in both the solo and choral contexts:

> The subjects were singers who were experienced both as choral singers and as soloists. In other words, it could be assumed that they were skilled in using their voices in both ways. In the case of the male subjects, pairs of tones sung at the same pitch, on the same vowel, and with the same loudness were compared. In the solo situation, each singer had a louder singer's formant and

slightly softer overtones below about 500Hz. In the case of the female subjects, long-term-average spectra were used to evaluate the result. The subjects had louder high overtones when they sang as soloists.[16]

This information would seem to indicate that the singers' formant functions more optimally in the solo situation than in the choral one.

More recent scientific research (2005) complicates the picture even further. In a study involving singers from the *Opera Australia* opera chorus, scientists analyzed the differences in vocal timbre between solo and choral singing modes: "The main finding was that there was similar or more relative energy in the higher frequency range, where the singer's formant occurs, in chorus mode when compared with solo singing mode."[17]

Intriguingly, this finding seems to contradict the older (Rossing) study, which found *less* energy in the singers' formant region during choral singing. But the studies may not contradict each other when genre and vocal training are taken into consideration.

It seems there is a scientific phenomenon in the choral environment whereby untrained singers use a brighter voice quality and trained singers tend to dampen their voices. Why? "It was concluded that individual singers used this dampening technique to achieve choral blend, and therefore, a different mode of production was needed for choral singing."[18]

Another interesting point made in the *Opera Australia* study is that voice teachers were less concerned for their solo singers when those singers were in an opera chorus as opposed to a choral ensemble.[19]

In short, the *Opera Australia* study conclusively demonstrated that when singing in an opera chorus, these subjects used a vocal timbre similar to that used in their solo singing. This is an incredible finding, but must be tempered by the fact that an opera chorus is very different than a choral ensemble.

Sundberg states that the center frequency of the singers' formant is low in basses and high in tenors. Then he asks,

> What happens to these formant frequency differences in a good choir? Do the members compromise so that all choir members agree on approximately the same formant frequencies, or do all section colleagues arrive at such an agreement, or is this an unimportant factor?[20]

These complex acoustics issues of the singers' formant and formant frequencies touch upon every nuance of the choral environment. Clearly voice science has much to tell us about how the solo voice functions in the choral setting. Hopefully, as technology advances, additional studies can be conducted on this important topic.

Notes

1. See the section "The Lombard Effect," later in this chapter.

2. Ingo Titze, personal interview with the author, December, 2000.

3. Johan Sundberg, *The Science of the Singing Voice* (Dekalb: Northern Illinois University Press, 1987), 140.

4. Sundberg, *The Science of the Singing Voice*, 140.

5. Johan Sundberg, "To Perceive One's Own Voice and Another Person's Voice," *Research Aspects on Singing* (1981): 84.

6. Allen W. Goodwin, "An Acoustical Study of Individual Voices in Choral Blend," *Journal of Research in Singing and Applied Vocal Pedagogy* 23 (1989): 25–34.

7. Sten Ternström, "Physical and Acoustic Factors That Interact with the Singer to Produce the Choral Sound," *Journal of Voice* 5 (1991): 128–42.

8. Ternström, "Physical and Acoustic Factors," 128–43.

9. Ternström, "Physical and Acoustic Factors," 133.

10. Louis H. Diercks and E. Milton Boone, "The Individual in the Choral Situation," *The NATS Bulletin* 17 (May 1961): 7.

11. Ternström, "Physical and Acoustic Factors," 133.

12. Ternström, "Physical and Acoustic Factors," 133.

13. Steven Tonkinson, "The Lombard Effect in Choral Singing," *Journal of Voice* 8 (1994): 24.

14. Tonkinson, "The Lombard Effect in Choral Singing," 28.

15. Sundberg, *The Science of the Singing Voice*, 145.

16. Sundberg, *The Science of the Singing Voice*, 141.

17. Katherine L. P. Reid, Pamela Davis, Jennifer Oates, Densil Cabrera, Sten Ternström, Michael Black, and Janice Chapman, "The Acoustic Characteristics of Professional Opera Singers Performing in Chorus Versus Solo Mode," *Journal of Voice* 21 (2007): 35.

18. Reid et al., "The Acoustic Characteristics of Professional Opera Singers," 40.

19. Reid et al., "The Acoustic Characteristics of Professional Opera Singers," 41.

20. Sundberg, *The Science of the Singing Voice*, 145.

CHAPTER TEN

~

Group *Vocalises*
for the Choral Rehearsal

Choral conductors have much to accomplish during the warm-up portion of the choral rehearsal. They must prepare all the voices in the group to handle the demands of the repertoire, and must vocally unite the group in terms of timbre, intonation, and intention.

Since a choir is made up of individual voices, it makes sense to use the same categories of vocal exercises that solo singers use. The choral conductor who adapts these *vocalises* for the group will benefit the vocal production of all the singers in the ensemble. The categories of vocal technique outlined in this chapter, and the order in which *vocalises* are presented, will assure the best possible vocal health for the ensemble singers.

The exercises in this chapter are grouped under the following *vocalise* categories: onset, glides or slides, increasing resonance, agility, vowel differentiation, *sostenuto*, unifying registers, range extension, and dynamic control. Suggestions as to how conductors can construct their own exercises are also offered.

Onset

The purpose of the onset exercise is to start the voice working. The short duration of these exercises ensures that the voice is not overtaxed too soon in the warm-up process. Onset exercises coordinate the instrument quickly, and begin to engage the abdominal musculature or support mechanism.

Onset exercises should be executed swiftly with the *tessitura* in the low, lower middle, and middle voice. An open, more neutral vowel (such as [a] or [open o]) is generally preferable to a closed tongue or lip-rounding vowel (such as [i] or [e]). However, some singers choose to start the voice on a closed vowel. Perhaps the best option is to alternate vowels. Encouraging singers to use "energy" and their "whole body" will promote coordination, while suggestions to "release" or "feel easy" will encourage external muscle release, preventing hyperfunction or oversinging. It may be beneficial to have the different sections of the ensemble alternate triads, so that fewer voices are heard at once and singers can be more closely observed.

Onsets for Group Warm-up 1

Divide the ensemble into sections (soprano, alto, tenor, bass) and alternate triads among each section. Voices move up by half steps to the middle voice and back down again. Vowels can change, but should be open or neutral. Singers use the [i] and [a] vowels with an "m" inserted at the beginning. At the beginning of phonation on each pitch, conductors may choose to make a hand gesture—perhaps a small motion of the hand sweeping outward. Such a gesture could reinforce the freedom of tone:

Onsets for Group Warm-up 2

The ensemble moves up and down by half steps, using a *staccato* attack:

Glides or Slides

Gliding, or sliding, through pitches within a limited range is an effective and fun way to begin vocalizing the voice. Gliding is not the same as singing a *glissando* or *portamento* in the context of an operatic aria; it is more about "making sound" than "full singing." A gliding exercise is a "stretch" for the vocal cords, which become elongated, but without heavy phonation.

When leading sliding exercises, the conductor should be careful not to use the extreme low or high of any vocal range. The focus should be on the middle register, as the voice should not move to its outer ends before it is properly warmed. Use of different vowels is fine, though many singers find the lip-rounding [u] vowel too restrictive in this exercise. The [i] vowel works very well for many singers.

Keep in mind that some singers may not have used slides in their individual practice or lessons, so it may take a little time for the ensemble to become comfortable with this exercise.

If conductors are feeling adventurous, they might try this exercise in the *falsetto* register with male singers. A sectional rehearsal may be the most appropriate place to try this for the first time. Most men should be able to access this register, although they may be uncomfortable with the sound they produce. Lower-voiced singers may have used the *falsetto* register for integrating their upper and middle voices in solo practice.

Slides for Group Warm-up, Women and Men

Singers should start in the lower middle voice and move upward and back down by half steps. Reminders to "release" and "move through the pitches" will help singers:

Increasing Resonance

The purpose of resonance exercises is to increase the resonance, or ringing, in the voice. Richard Miller refers to this concept as "resonance balance." Perhaps Miller's term is more scientifically sound, but "increasing resonance" and "resonance balance" essentially refer to the same issue.[1]

Resonance in the voice is a complex issue, especially because singers interpret their own resonance in different ways, and some singers have more nasality than others. See chapters one and three for specific discussions of resonance. It may help to think of resonance as "ring," and resonance exercises as increasing "ring" in the voice.

Conductors will have to find out which vocal sounds best bring out the resonance balance in their ensembles, but the "hum" and the consonant cluster "ng" are commonly used in solo singing. As mentioned in chapter three, voice scientists have revealed that when singers create a resistance to airflow, as in humming, sounds are better balanced with regard to resonance quality.

Humming exercises are efficient since they provide singers with a perfect opportunity to check themselves for nasality or lack of resonance. Moreover, humming does not utilize the entire vocal fold and is not as taxing as full phonation. Humming is a "quiet" exercise for beginning a rehearsal and heightening the singers' awareness of functioning as part of a group.

Conductors asking questions of singers before and after a resonance exercise can facilitate this awareness. Such questions might include: "Did you feel an increase in space?" "Where are you sensing the resonance of your voice?" or "Where do you feel the vibrations?"

Conductors who are particularly interested in resonance balance may want to explore additional exercises that apply nasopharyngeal occlusion (closed nostrils). The main point of these exercises is that a singer's sense of resonance and awareness is increased with nostrils closed.

Increasing Resonance in the Group Warm-up 1

This is a non-singing exercise, and a good one to use regularly in rehearsal. The concept is that singers will create more space in the pharynx and vocal tract by the inner lifting that happens naturally when inhaling a pleasant scent. The conductor should give the ensemble the following instructions, repeating the exercise as needed:

1. Stand in a noble posture and ready to sing, with shoulders relaxed, knees flexible, and the sternum in a lifted and tall position, but not raised.
2. Close your eyes.
3. Inhale very slowly, imagining you are smelling something pleasant.
4. Be aware of the lift of your soft palate and the increased vertical space you feel inside your mouth.
5. Release the breath slowly.

Increasing Resonance in the Group Warm-up 2

This exercise teaches singers how to distinguish between a resonant and non-resonant "hum." Have the singers spread out considerably so that they are at least two feet apart. Singers "hum" on any comfortable pitch. Midway through the pitch, have them "flip" their bottom lip quickly with their forefinger. If they are humming "in resonance," a small sound will emit from their lips. If they are not singing "in resonance" but "in nasality," no sound will emit from the lips. Singers should be able to tell if they are in resonance or nasality immediately.

Obviously it is preferable that singers "hum" in resonance for an optimal vocal tone. The conductor may need to demonstrate this exercise for the singers before they give it a try. After the exercise, the conductor should ascertain how many singers hummed in resonance. Singers not in resonance should practice outside of rehearsal until they can "hum" in resonance.

Increasing Resonance in the Group Warm-up 3

Once the ensemble can "hum" in resonance, the conductor can move on to this exercise. Have the singers "hum" on a descending five-note scale while sensing the resonance. (Singers can always check themselves by "flipping" their bottom lip at any point in the exercise.) Singers move up and back down by half steps using mostly the middle voice. Singers should stop humming if the *tessitura* becomes too high. Conductors can remind singers to keep a feeling of vertical space inside the mouth, and to have "loose lips" that are "completely closed, but not tight."

Increasing Resonance in the Group Warm-up 4

This exercise is also sung on a descending five-note scale, but mixes in the vowel [a] so that singers can transfer resonance directly from a "hum" to a sung vowel. Singers move up and down by half steps:

Increasing Resonance in the Group Warm-up 5

This exercise is the opposite of the "hum" exercises, in that the vibrations should be felt in the nasal area, not the lips. The tongue is raised to the hard palate and completely closes the pharynx, forcing the singer to sense resonance in the nasopharanx instead of the mouth and lips. This exercise uses the consonant cluster "ng" and may feel uncomfortable at first:

Increasing Resonance in the Group Warm-up 6

This exercise mixes the "ng" sound used in the exercise above with the vowel [a]. Singers should sense a dramatic increase in resonance perception—and a real opening up of the pharyngeal space—when moving from the "ng" to the [a] vowel:

ng - a - ng - a - ng   ng - a - ng - a - ng   ng - a - ng - a - ng

a - ng - a - ng - a   a - ng - a - ng - a   a - ng - a - ng - a

Agility

Agility in singing, especially choral singing, is an essential part of the vocal technique. Agility exercises may be neglected in the choral environment because they are very difficult to coordinate with more than one singer. The purpose of the agility exercise is to increase the ability of the voice to sing musical phrases that have a lot of movement or move quickly. Vocal agility is particularly necessary for phrases that encompass *coloratura* and *fioritura* (runs), for example.

When conductors are constructing exercises for agility, they should consider the repertoire demands of the ensemble. For example, if an ensemble is performing G. F. Handel's *Messiah* in December, the conductor could teach certain quick-moving passages of "For Unto Us a Child Is Born" in September, and include those passages in the regular warm-up. It might be interesting for the sections of the ensemble to exchange parts; the tenors could sing the bass passage, and the altos could sing the tenor passage, for example. In this way, the singers could approach the passages as an exercise only, outside the context of the piece. If these passages are practiced regularly as warm-ups, the required agility will be well-ingrained in the singers' muscle memory by December.

There is no limitation to what conductors can try if they focus on agility passages as *exercises*, and not as a musical rehearsal. Regular focus on these exercises will improve the ensemble's agility and the vocal dexterity of each individual.

In general, agility exercises should be practiced in the low, middle, and upper voice in order to accommodate all the demands of the choral literature.

Agility Exercise for Group Warm-up 1

Singers follow the five-note scale below, moving up and down by half steps, and using different vowels. Start with one scale, and as singers become more comfortable, increase to two scales, and then three scales. Sections can sing individually and alternate scales. Women and men should sing in the most appropriate octave for them. It may be useful to progress from closed tongue vowels to closed lip vowels; [i] to [e] to [a] to [o] to [u], for example. Conductors can have the ensemble sing the exercise with vowels only or with a "v" in front of the vowels. The voiced fricative "v" promotes adduction (vocal fold closure) and a neutral tongue position:

Agility Exercise for Group Warm-up 2

This exercise can be sung on any vowel, or vowels can be alternated at the start of each phrase. For example, singers can alternate between [i] and [e] or [a] and [o]. Conductors can remind singers to "think of the phrase as one note." If the tone is sluggish or the breath energy is low, singers should be reminded to "move the air" or "increase the breath energy." The "h" sound should not be heard in-between pitches:

Agility Exercise for Group Warm-up 3

This is an advanced exercise, and use of any vowel is acceptable. Singers will need to have plenty of breath energy and vertical pharyngeal space at the start of each phrase:

Vowel Differentiation

The purpose of the vowel differentiation exercise is to fuse vowel clarity with vocal technique. Sung vowels must be clear in order to be understood. The pure vowel sounds must be established before the ensemble moves on to mixed or nasal vowels. If the ensemble can produce a clear and pure vowel sound, it is well on its way to singing text that is easily understood by the audience. Since vowel sounds vary according to the *tessitura* in use, these exercises should be practiced in the low, middle, and upper registers for both women and men. When constructing vowel differentiation exercises, conductors should consider which language to focus on at a particular rehearsal.

The conductor should go through the piece, write down every vowel sung, and then make a list of the vowels sung by each voice part in the low, middle, and high registers. The last chorus in Felix Mendelssohn's *Elijah*, "And Then Shall Your Light Break Forth," shall serve as an example. For the sopranos, [u] "you" and the last syllable of [open o] "nations" are sung in the low voice; [open o] and [I] "morning," [open e] and [ə] "ever," and [aːe] "thy" are sung in the middle voice; and [e] "name," [open e] "heav'n," and [a] "amen" are sung in the top voice.

The conductor then compares all the voice parts, noting any similarity in the vowels sung by each part. In the Mendelssohn piece, for example, all the voice parts sing [a] and [aːe] in the middle voice. The conductor can then construct vowel exercises in the middle voice for the entire ensemble, using the vowels sung in this particular movement of the oratorio. Another option is to have each section individually sing certain vowels in the different tessituras; for example, the altos alone would sing vowels in their low, middle, and top voice.

Yet another option is to have one section sing certain diphthongs while the other sections listen for clarity. The isolation of sections during the vocalizing process may take more time, but the conductor can better scrutinize the output of each section, and the result will be greater vowel clarity from the complete ensemble.

Vowel Differentiation Exercise for Group Warm-up 1

Sing the descending five-note scale, alternating the tongue vowels [i] and [e], the open vowels [a] and [open o], and the closed lip-rounding vowels [o] and [u]. (These vowel combinations do not have to be executed all on the same day.) Move up and down by half steps.

vi - e - i - e - i   va - ɔ - a - ɔ - a   vo - u - o - u - o

vi - e - i - e - i   va - ɔ - a - ɔ - a   vo - u - o - u - o

va - ɔ - a - ɔ - a   vi - e - i - e - i   va - ɔ - a - ɔ - a

Vowel Differentiation Exercise for Group Warm-up 2

The ensemble moves up and down by half steps. Conductors should listen for vowel clarity, and if they don't hear it, they can isolate the sections:

Sostenuto

The purpose of a *sostenuto* or sustained exercise is to maximize *legato* and practice breath management. Singers should focus on their inhalation and exhalation during these exercises, and ideally the conductor should know how to convey the principles of good breath management in clear language to the ensemble.

When planning a *sostenuto* exercise, conductors should consider how challenging these *vocalises* ought to be. The ensemble can start with short phrases and build up to much longer phrases as they gain breath control.

Conductors should listen for the integrity of the vowels. During the execution of the phrase, singers can migrate from the original vowel into a diphthong if they are not careful.

Sostenuto Exercise for Group Warm-up 1

These exercises may be sung up or down the fifth interval. Inhalation should be complete and efficient; in other words, inhalation should be deep, low, and wide, with the upper chest, shoulders, and head held still for the duration:

Sostenuto Exercise for Group Warm-up 2

The ensemble moves up and down by half steps. Singers should connect every pitch with breath for a complete *legato* tone. If singers run out of air before a phrase is complete, they may be letting air escape too quickly:

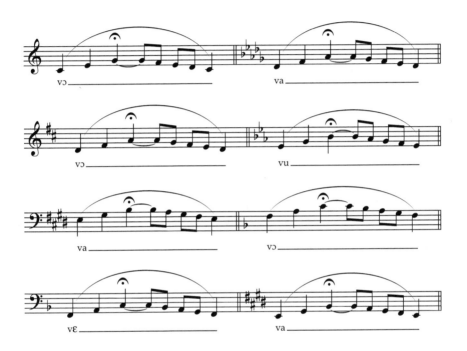

Sostenuto Exercise for Group Warm-up 3

This exercise is more difficult than the previous ones because it incorporates an octave leap and requires faster airflow. The ensemble moves up and down by half steps. The conductor can have singers alternate exercises, or have the lower voices drop out if needed:

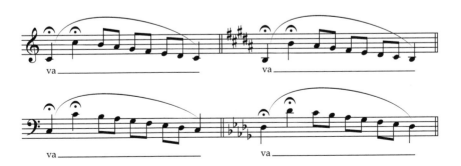

Unifying Registers

The purpose of register unification exercises is to create as uniform a sound as possible throughout all registers of the voice. As previously discussed, certain zones of the voice are transition (*passaggio*) areas where the voice moves from one register to another. Vocal registration is a highly nuanced issue that is greatly dependent on the individual needs of the singer.

In the choral setting, a conductor can utilize certain register exercises that apply to most singers. Rarely used registers and a singer's individual issues cannot be addressed in choral rehearsals, but exercises that move the ensemble's voices among registers *can* be introduced.

The best time to employ these exercises is probably during the sectional rehearsal, where the focus can be on the male or female voice exclusively. The conductor should determine the *primo* and *secondo passaggio* for the male and female voices and plan exercises accordingly. These transition points vary according to different sources, and more information is available in vocal pedagogy texts (see bibliography).

In general, register unification exercises should either start *below* a transition point and ascend above it, or start just *above* a transition point and descend below it.[2]

The next two examples demonstrate a register exercise for the mezzo-soprano (Alto I) and baritone (Bass) voices.

Register Exercise for the Group Warm-up (Alto I)
The mezzo-sopranos (Alto I) should sing the fifth interval on the [a] vowel. The first transition point is identified as F4 and the second transition point is identified as E5. This exercise is written in the treble clef for clarity, but can be transposed for any vocal category:

Register Exercise for the Baritone Voice (Bass I)
The baritones should sing the fifth interval on the [open o] vowel. The first transition point is identified as B4 and the second transition point is identified as E4:[3]

Register Exercise for the Group Warm-up 1

The ensemble sings octave leaps, moving up and down by half steps:

Register Exercise for the Group Warm-up 2

The ensemble sings the downward fifth, first on a slide and then on the [a] vowel:

Range Extension

Range extension exercises are designed to extend both the top and bottom range of the singer. These exercises also keep the extremes of the range in good shape.

When constructing these exercises, the conductor may want to focus on the tenor and soprano sections, since they regularly sing in the higher *tessituras*. When working with the altos, the conductor may want to work downward into the lower range (chest voice), since most women need to strengthen this part of the voice. Basses can also work on extending and strengthening their lower range. Range extension exercises are particularly demanding and should thus be included at the end of the warm-up.

Range Extension Exercise for the Group Warm-up 1

The ensemble sings the *arpeggios* up and down by half steps. Singers should focus on their abdominal connection on each pitch, as well as vertical space in the pharynx (inside the mouth):

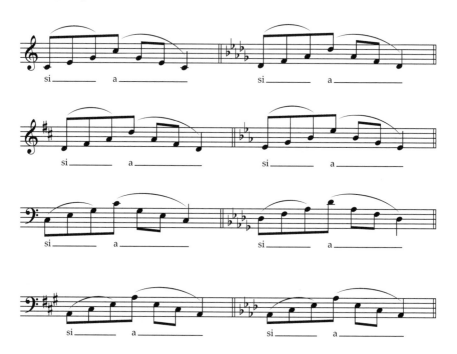

Range Extension Exercise for the Group Warm-up 2

The ensemble sings the *staccato arpeggios* up and down by half steps. Singers should drop out if they are uncomfortable or unable to sing any higher or lower:

Range Extension Exercise for the Group Warm-up 3
The ensemble sings the scales up and down by half steps:

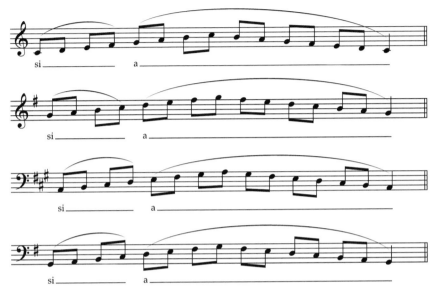

Dynamic Control

Control of dynamics is one of the most challenging aspects of voice production. Singing softly requires an advanced level of coordination and does not come easily to many singers whose vocal technique is not solidified. The most common exercise for dynamic control is the *messa di voce* (middle of the voice) which consists of a gradual *crescendo* and a slow *decrescendo* on a single pitch.

When constructing these exercises, the conductor will want to consider the demands of dynamics within the literature performed by the choir. A dynamically difficult section of a certain piece can be transformed into an exercise. The conductor can choose the measures that need attention, isolate the vowels that are sung, and have the choir sing the section just on those vowels. It is not necessary to keep the performance tempo for this exercise. When the choir is ready, add the consonants for complete text but remain out of performance tempo. This kind of practice should promote strong muscle memory in the singers and a much more exciting, dynamically varied voice production.

Dynamic control exercises should include the higher *tessituras*, since they are the most challenging for singers to sing softly. However, it is preferable to start in the middle or low voice and work upward.

Dynamic Control Exercise for Group Warm-up 1

This exercise is known as *messa di voce*. Any vowel can be used, but keep in mind that in high *tessituras* closed vowels are more challenging than open vowels. The same dynamic should not last more than one beat; in other words, the tone is constantly moving from soft to loud and loud to soft:

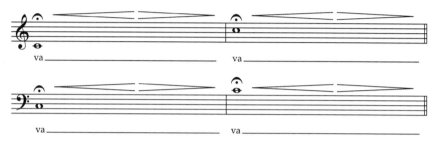

Dynamic Control Exercise for Group Warm-up 2

This exercise is very fun and can alternate soprano, alto, tenor, and bass voices. The conductor can have sections alternate triads or individual pitches. The exercise requires quick dynamic shifts, coordination, and abdominal support:

Dynamic Control Exercise for Group Warm-up 3

This exercise is almost the same as the previous one, except that more than one vowel is utilized. Conductors can use any vowels they choose:

Regular use of these suggested exercises, which cover all aspects of vocal technique and are congruent with vocal health, can supplement the conductor's regular warm-up routine. Conductors should feel free to make any adjustments they feel are necessary to best serve their ensemble's needs.

Notes

1. Richard Miller, *The Structure of Singing: System and Art in Vocal Technique* (New York: Schirmer Books, 1996), 62.

2. Miller, *The Structure of Singing*, 126.

3. Miller, *The Structure of Singing*, 117, 135.

Conclusion

At the time of this publication, no conclusive scientific studies had been conducted on the long-term effects of choral participation on the solo singer's voice. Questions to consider in future research include: At what point are solo voices negatively affected by volume control, repetition, and vocal duration in choir? What are the principle criteria for determining whether any such effects are negative? How can the solo singer best balance choral participation with solo singing?

What is certain is that choral singing can present challenges for solo singers. The choral singing environment can affect the way a solo singer stands and sits, as well as vibrato rate, breath flow, tonal placement, vocal timbre, vowel shape, placement of consonants, and foreign language pronunciation. The singer must work with a group, rather than individually; deal with the voice production of other singers as well as his own; and follow the musical interpretation of the conductor.

It is reasonable to conclude that the simultaneous practice of choral and solo technique entails certain vocal demands that the young singer, especially, will be unaware of and unable to handle. Some singers will have difficulty reconciling personal goals with collective goals, self-motivation with the conductor's leadership, and individual color and feeling with modification and blend. It must be conceded that a solo singer's vocal progress and development could potentially be delayed by the diversion of their vocal energy to the choral environment.

On the other hand, the collegiate choral experience has much to offer. For most vocal majors, a solo singing career is not a realistic probability. Experience in choir will offer career options for singers and expand their worldview. Many college-age solo singers greatly enjoy the choral experience. They feel a sense of camaraderie with other students, without the performance anxiety they might experience in a solo context. Learning to listen to others while singing is essential for any singer participating in an operatic or oratorio work. Exposure to the choral repertoire of major composers is also essential to the young singer.

The solutions offered in this text are suggestive in nature. Both singer and conductor may find that some of these solutions work well and others don't. If problems persist and all else fails, conductors should concede that a singer's decision *not* to sing during a choral rehearsal is a valid choice. Sometimes, to preserve the voice, "dropping out" is a singer's only option. Some choral conductors, including Hugh Ferguson Floyd and Timothy Stalter, agree with this principle. They may not prefer "dropping out" as a solution to vocal challenges, but as conductors they understand singers have limits.

James McKinney has the following advice for the singer:

> He should have the wisdom to protect his own voice by dropping the octave when the notes lie too high or by just faking it—pretending to sing. It is *his* voice he is hurting, not the director's![1]

Singers participating in the choral ensemble are not advised to "fake it," but at the same time, they cannot always meet the ensemble's every demand. Conductors will win the admiration and respect of their singers if they can reconcile themselves to the fact that singers must sometimes conserve their voices. Responsibility also rests on solo singers to participate fully in choir whenever they are vocally able, so that when they do need to rest, the conductor is empathetic.

It is up to the individual singer to weigh the benefits of choral singing against the potential risks and distractions. The choral requirement is greatly emphasized in the vocal curriculum of the typical American liberal arts college and university. The young singer has the option of attending a music conservatory for formal study, thereby avoiding the choral requirement altogether. However, students who wish to obtain a well-rounded liberal arts education as a vocal major will most certainly find themselves in a choir. Curriculum changes that demand less time of the vocal major in a choral setting may reduce possible vocal risks.

Close interaction and communication among students, voice faculty, and choral faculty will benefit everyone involved. Collegiality, empathy, and knowledge of voice science will empower teachers of singing and choral conductors as they continue to search for a balance of singing disciplines.

Note

1. James C. McKinney, *The Diagnosis and Correction of Vocal Faults* (Nashville, TN: Genevox Music Group, 1994), 119.

~

Appendix: Conversations with Two Choral Conductors

Dr. Melinda O'Neal

What is one of the most challenging aspects of choral conducting in regard to dealing with trained solo singers?

It depends a great deal on the size of the ensemble and the repertoire. For a small ensemble, the most important challenge has been to find solo singers whose voices are relatively well-matched in weight and color, and who are comparable in skill. When the singers mutually respect each other, the personality dynamics work very well. But with wide variances in skills, vowels, colors, pitches, and volume, disgruntled attitudes emerge which become detrimental to the musical results. With larger ensembles, again, issues of weight and color are still evident. It's important to locate the more distinctive, larger voices in each section so that the most reliable ones are centrally located and/or evenly distributed, so as to act as an anchor for the entire section's sound. I like to have a vocal section with a well-matched, but distinctive color rather than a median-like, compromised (sometimes called "blended") sound. Trained soloists in an ensemble are key to gaining distinctive character in the corporate sound.

Is there an instance in rehearsal or performance where you notice a difference between the solo singers and the choral singers?

I like to think of singers as singers. Everyone should be able to sing by himself or herself and everyone should relish the opportunity to sing in an ensemble if the repertoire is good and the ensemble is well led. Some singers have more training, a more distinctive sound, greater agility, or more weight than others. But they are all human beings and ensemble citizens, and I address them as such.

How much do the attitudes of the vocal majors you work with influence the success of your ensemble?

I have found that the more accomplished singers enjoy the ensemble experience because they know they gain literacy, musicianship, and opportunity, plus—and simply put—it is profoundly enjoyable to sing with others. Their positive attitude influences others who may feel lesser-skilled. It's my job as a conductor to create an atmosphere where all singers are respected and appreciated, no matter the quality of their vocal contribution or level of skill. They all must be inspired by the music to do their best. Approaches or techniques employed in an ensemble situation that leave some singers feeling extraneous or inadequate—or others feeling superior or the exception to the rule—are absolutely inappropriate.

Do you try to incorporate any vocal pedagogy into the choral rehearsal?

The greater the skill set and better the sound of an ensemble—that is, the more I like what I'm hearing—the less I address pedagogy. I ask for a different vowel or color or line or affect from highly skilled singers rather than advise on technique. I address everything on the basis of the demands of the music and text as per my interpretation. The more variable the musical result and/or the lesser the skill set of an ensemble, the more necessary it is to work through vocal pedagogy to achieve desired results.

How do you deal with singers who have severe vocal deficiencies?

I don't select them to sing in my ensemble. If they develop vocal difficulties during the term, I take them aside to work with them individually. If they are at the verge of vocal distress, I ask to hear them individually and then advise them not to sing while they obtain qualified help. Singers usually are aware when they are not singing well and they appreciate being dealt with honestly.

Have you had to ask older singers to leave your ensemble?

Yes, and it's very difficult. Most singers, however, understand the performance ideals and standards of the organization. The imperative for the organization to deliver an outstanding musical product supercedes the imperative to provide a singing opportunity for a member who is not a positive contribution. I re-audition singers each year and deal individually with each person. I speak in terms of their overall physical health (diet, exercise, sleep, stress management) and then their vocal health. Usually singers who have sung with good technique over the years will have good longevity of vocal health. Those who have carried poor singing habits with them for years do not have late-life staying power. Overall muscular coordination in the process of supporting and making the sound are compromised so that pitch, agility, and tone are affected. A mature person will usually know what category they fit in. On occasion, though, a singer is not ready or willing to face realities; this is always unfortunate and very difficult for all concerned. Changes in our bodies, however, are an inevitable component of the human condition.

How do you feel about singers dropping out of passages that are particularly hard for them vocally?

This approach has never occurred to me. For more florid passages in Baroque music or to achieve more transparency in the sound, I have often used the *concertist-ripienist* approach. This entails planning from the outset to designate a smaller ensemble to sing a particular passage for a special effect.

What suggestions do you have for vocal majors who must sing in choir, lessons, classes, opera, etc.? How can they cover all these demands in a given day?

Pace themselves, as they must preserve their vocal capital. Rest some of the time so as to be ready for other moments when their voice is more exposed or more important. Speak to the teacher, director, or conductor before class to advise them of vocal fatigue, etc., if a problem is anticipated. Clearly singers should not enroll in so many courses such that physical/vocal demands exceed their capacity to function in a positive way.

What are the most important expectations you have of your singers?

They must care first and foremost for the music, as I do. That they have the desire to serve the music and composer's aesthetic intent more than anything else. Following this, maintain good health and vocal readiness, prepare difficult passages outside of rehearsal, be a leader rather than a follower at all times, be on time.

In your career have you found relationships with voice faculty comfortable? Is the issue of the solo singer in the choral setting discussed in a positive way?

In my experience there usually is a prevailing philosophy in a voice department about ensemble singing that is either generally positive or generally negative. The approach of the choral conductor has the most influence on voice teachers' attitudes. Most voice teachers recognize that ensemble experiences provide improved literacy and musicianship as well as offer opportunities for emerging soloists to gain experience and attention. Teachers also recognize that their students are works-in-progress, and the wise ones advise their students to earn their way and be patient if they seek solo opportunities through the ensemble. As long as the choral conductor a) does not misuse singers' voices (over-manipulate, over-fatigue); b) does not abuse singers' integrity or sense of self-respect; c) pays attention to the improvements in his or her singers; d) uses good judgment in selecting repertoire well-suited to the ensemble's skills; and e) applies good judgment in selecting singers fairly and openly for solo roles, I've found voice teacher and conductor relationships to be mutually beneficial. The best music departments are those in which the teachers and conductors keep an open dialogue and work together for the benefit of the students' progress.

Thank you, Dr. O'Neal!

Biography of Dr. Melinda O'Neal

Dr. Melinda O'Neal is currently the conductor and musical director of the Handel Choir of Baltimore. She is co-founder and conductor of Sonique, Boston Vocal Artists' ten-voice professional chamber ensemble, and professor of music at Dartmouth College in Hanover, New Hampshire. From 1979 to 2004 O'Neal was music director and conductor of the Handel Society of Dartmouth College. O'Neal holds master's and doctoral degrees in choral-orchestral conducting from Indiana University in Bloomington and a bachelors in music education from Florida State University in Tallahassee. She studied score preparation, choral literature, and conducting with Julius Herford, Jan Harrington, Fiora Contino, Helmuth Rilling, Robert Shaw, Marcel Couraud, John Nelson, and Thomas Dunn. At Dartmouth College O'Neal teaches courses in conducting, studies in music and text, and music theory. O'Neal is a past board member of the Conductors Guild and serves on the research and publications committee of the American Choral Directors Association.

Dr. Timothy Stalter

What is one of the most challenging aspects of choral conducting in regard to dealing with trained solo singers?

Being a trained, solo singer myself, I am very supportive of these voices in my choirs. Most of the time I find these singers to be excellent people with whom to work. What I do not like to find in a trained or untrained singer is an unwillingness to love the music more than one's own voice, an ideal introduced to me by the late Robert Shaw. I feel the same with people who sing or play an instrument—their passion for the music must supersede their love for their instrument, which is simply a means of conveying their love for the music. Another more practical concern that crops up from time to time is articulation. Again, both trained and untrained singers (and instrumentalists) can have difficulty understanding how articulation informs the stylistic qualities of the music. We have a tendency to train singers to sing more in the Romantic style—longer lines with ultimate connectivity—which a solo singer may be able to get by with, no matter what style or piece. However, there are times when this is not the ideal and this more Romantic singing actually does not serve the music well (Baroque dance music, for instance). Again, this is not limited to trained singers.

Is there an instance in rehearsal or performance where you notice a difference between the solo singers and the choral singers?

I would suggest that when solo singers sing in a choral ensemble they are choral singers. I make no distinction. Choral singing is a skill with which all singers must have experience. Many (not all, but many) singers who hope to sing professionally might need to sing in an ensemble at some point in their careers. So, I must admit, I do not really make a distinction between the "solo singer" and the "choral singer." They function as one and the same for me.

How much do the attitudes of the vocal majors you work with influence the success of your ensemble?

All singers in a choir need to contribute positively to an ensemble. Any member, solo singer or not, can influence the success of an ensemble. I have not found one to be more problematic than the other.

Do you try to incorporate any vocal pedagogy into the choral rehearsal?

Yes, I ask that the singers exhibit good singing posture whether they are sitting or standing, that they sing in the core of their sound, and that they exhibit a healthy sound through excellent breath management. I also work on vowel formation and timbre. Now, I will be the first to admit that working with registration and timbre should best be left to one-on-one teaching in the voice studio. However, I will state that there are a number of things which can be taught en masse.

How do you deal with singers who have severe vocal deficiencies?
If you are asking about pathological problems (nodes, etc.), I refer them immediately to our excellent voice clinic here at the University of Iowa. I give them the rest they need as prescribed by their doctor. I do not practice medicine, but I do hear voices which are in trouble and am very sensitive not to allow further damage.

Have you had to ask older singers to leave your ensemble?
If by older, you mean singers who have been singing for a number of years and have returned for advanced degrees in voice, then I have never asked these singers to leave my ensemble except when they have not been attending rehearsals as described in our choral grading policies. If you mean asking a singer to leave because of how large or mature their voice is—not always synonymous, I must be quick to add—then I would say there have been very few cases when I did not have an ensemble to suit a particular voice. In those cases I made alternate arrangements so as not to frustrate the singer.

How do you feel about singers dropping out of passages that are particularly hard for them vocally?
I feel perfectly fine about it.

What suggestions do you have for vocal majors who must sing in choir, lessons, classes, opera, etc.? How can they cover all these demands in a given day?
Do not sing high and loud all day long. Learn to manage your singing day, how to "mark" properly and efficiently. This is a fact of a singer's life. I have purposefully spread out my rehearsals throughout the week, making shorter rehearsal times precisely for this reason. I find that certain singers need to sing *fortissimo* all the time, a practice which can be detrimental in the long run, not to mention the fact that they are not cultivating as rich a spectrum of dynamic level as is demanded by a number of composers who write for solo voices.

What are the most important expectations you have of your singers?
Care for the music and develop an instrument which can serve it admirably.

In your career have you found relationships with voice faculty comfortable? Is the issue of the solo singer in the choral setting discussed in a positive way?

I find my relationships with the voice faculty to be very comfortable and amiable. I enjoy working with voice teachers very much and seek opportunities to do more with them. I am very supportive of their work. I know that problems do arise now and then about where a student is placed or certain vocal concerns; however, open dialogue with both students and teachers is essential and necessary in order for the student to come through these difficulties. I want to work with the studio, not against it, and make this perfectly clear to the students at the beginning of each new year.

Thank you, Dr. Stalter!

Biography of Dr. Timothy Stalter

Dr. Timothy Stalter is director of choral activities at the University of Iowa and conducts Iowa's premiere choral ensemble, Kantorei, and summer opera. He also teaches graduate advanced conducting and administrates the graduate program in choral conducting. Before coming to Iowa, Dr. Stalter was assistant director of choral activities at the University of Wisconsin at Madison; director of choral activities at the University of Wisconsin at Stevens Point; and assistant professor of music at Goshen College.

He received his doctorate from the University of Wisconsin at Madison in choral conducting under Robert Fountain and is particularly interested in issues relating to historical musical performance and the teaching of conducting to undergraduates. He is a frequent guest clinician in the United States and is an active member of the American Choral Directors Association.

In addition to conducting and teaching choral music, Dr. Stalter is active as a tenor soloist in the United States and abroad, specializing in music of the Renaissance, Baroque, and Classical periods. He is widely known for his performances as the Evangelist in the *Passions* of J. S. Bach and Heinrich Schütz. Among his credits are appearances as tenor soloist with the Newfoundland Symphony Orchestra, the North Carolina Symphony, the Robert Shaw Festival Singers (in France), the Robert Shaw Chamber Choir (in Atlanta), the Classical Music Seminar and Festival (in Eisenstadt, Austria), and the Shenandoah Valley Bach Festival. In 1999, he was tenor soloist in Haydn's *Creation* for the International Cathedral Music Festival in Oxford and London, England. Dr. Stalter has also recorded as soloist with Robert Shaw on two compact discs, *Amazing Grace* and *Songs of Angels*, released on the Telarc label.

~

Glossary

a cappella: in modern-day usage, singing without accompaniment

abdominal musculature: the rectus sheath, the rectus abdominis, the external and internal obliques, and the transversus abdominis muscles, all of which facilitate the breath cycle and support the vocal mechanism

abduction: a moving apart of the vocal folds

adduction: a moving together of the vocal folds

alto: in modern-day usage, the low female part in a choral ensemble

appoggio: from the Italian *appoggiarsi* (to lean upon), a balance of musculature that ensures an efficient breath cycle and optimum vocal tone

aria: a song for solo voice from an opera

arpeggio: the execution of the notes of a chord in succession, instead of at the same time; often used in vocal exercises

articulators: the parts of the body that shape the vocal tract and articulate vowels and consonants; the soft palate, tongue, and lips

arytenoids: cartilages in the larynx that attach to the vocal folds

attack: the initial phonation or onset

baritone: a vocal classification for a male voice that is higher than the bass and lower than the tenor

bass: a vocal classification for the lowest male voice, and the choral classification for the lowest male voices in a choral ensemble

basso-profondo: a vocal classification used in solo singing for a male singer with a deep bass voice

bel canto: Italian for "beautiful singing"; a singing style often associated with nineteenth-century Italian operatic literature

blend: in choral singing, a state in which no individual voices are distinguishable

bone conduction: in singing, sensing of resonance through bone

breath cycle: the process of breathing in singing; the four stages consist of inhalation, suspension, exhalation, and recovery

breath management: how a person manages airflow for efficiency in singing; breath control

breath support: related to but not exactly breath management or abdominal support, this term means different things to different people; "breath energy" may be closest in meaning

bronchi: branches formed of cartilage that are attached to the trachea that transport air to the lungs

cartilage: a human connective tissue that is firm but more flexible and less hard than bone; within the larynx, the cricoid, thyroid, arytenoid, and epiglottis are made of cartilage

chest voice: a lower register of the human voice in which resonance is felt in and around the chest area; a register in which a heavy mechanism or more muscular action can be applied

classification: in singing, the process of placing a human voice in the correct vocal category

coloratura: the classification for the highest female voice; or, fast-moving musical passages that require vocal agility

concerto: a musical composition for one or more instruments, usually with orchestral accompaniment

consonant clusters: a grouping of more than one consonant at the beginning, middle, or end of a word; for example *pflantz* in German, or *gloria* in Italian

countertenor: in modern-day usage, a male singer who sings exclusively in his falsetto register

crescendo: in singing, a gradual increase in volume or dynamic level

cricoarytenoids: muscles within the larynx

cricoid: the ring-shaped cartilage at the base of the larynx

decibel: a unit that measures intensity of sound; abbreviated as "dB"

decrescendo: in singing, a gradual decrease in volume or dynamic level

diaphragm: the dome-shaped muscle that makes breathing possible and separates the thorax from the viscera

diction: in singing, the enunciation and pronunciation of vowels and consonants

diminuendo: a decrease in dynamic level

diphthong: two consecutive vowel sounds

diva/divo: an accomplished female/male singer

emotional substitution: an acting technique that uses real life experiences and emotional memories of a singer in the life of a character

en masse: as a body or in a group; from the French

epigastric region: the upper region of the abdominal area

epiglottis: a leaf-shaped cartilage attached to the larynx that covers the trachea during swallowing

esprit de corps: an attitude of commonality within a group of people

exhalation: the third stage of the breath cycle, in which phrases are sung

fach: German term referring to the European system of voice classification; also, a classification within that system

facial mask: in singing, any area in the face where a singer senses resonance

falsetto: a vocal register in the male voice, located above the typical upper register and not typically utilized in performance, except by countertenors

feedback: in acoustic science, the auditory sensation of one's own voice

fermata: Italian for "stop"; in a musical score, a notation that indicates where a singer may hold a note as long as he likes

fioritura: literally "flowering" from the Italian; runs or fast-moving passages in a vocal line

flageolet: a seldom-used register of the female voice that extends above the head voice; also known as the "whistle register"

flat: in singing, not centered and too low in pitch

formants: resonances that emit from the vocal tract

fortissimo: very loud

free tone: in singing, a state in which the voice is operating at an optimum level with free-flowing air, a released vocal mechanism, and resonance that produces overtones

fricative: a consonant produced by airflow passing through a narrow mouth opening; examples include [v], [f], and [z]

full voice: producing tone at the full level of a singer's capability

glissando: the act of sliding up or down a musical interval or scale

glottis: the space between the vocal folds

half voice: producing tone at less than a singer's full capability

head voice: producing tone in the top register; or, a singer's sensation of tone in the head

heavy mechanism: increased muscular tension in phonation, often employed in chest voice or to supplement dramatic intent

hyoid bone: a bone forming the top portion of the laryngeal structure; also known as the "lone bone" for being unattached to any other bone

hyperfunction: oversinging

imagery: in the teaching of singing, a technique that conveys technical concepts through images and impressions rather than scientifically based knowledge

infrahyoids: a group of extrinsic muscles that lower the larynx

inhalation: the process of taking air into the lungs; the first stage of the breathing cycle

inspiration: inhalation; taking in air

interarytenoids: intrinsic muscles of the larynx

intercostals: the muscles between the ribs

International Phonetic Alphabet (IPA): a system of symbols created by the International Phonetic Association and used by singers to correctly pronounce and sing foreign languages

intonation: accuracy of pitch in the production of music

isometric exercises: body movements that utilize antagonistic muscular action

laryngeal depressors: muscles that lower the larynx

laryngeal elevators: muscles that raise the larynx

laryngologist: a doctor who specializes in the care of the voice

larynx: the primary organ of sound production, located in the neck, at the top of the trachea, and containing the vocal folds; also known as the "voice box"

lead-ins: in choral singing, the place in the music immediately prior to the choir's entrance

legato: smooth and connected

lied: a German art song

Lombard effect: an acoustic phenomenon in which singers in the choral environment increase their volume in response to auditory feedback

marking: a practice in which a singer does not produce sound in full voice; or, a procedure employed by professional singers to minimize vocal use in rehearsal

mask: the frontal area of the face where singers can sense vibrations

messa di voce: "placing the voice" in Italian; a vocal exercise related to dynamic control

mezzo-soprano: a vocal category for women that is lower than soprano and higher than contralto

middle voice: the part of the voice that lies between the lowest and highest registers

mixed vowel: the pronunciation of two vowel sounds at the same time, using the tongue for one vowel and the shape of the lips for the other

modification: in singing, the alteration of one or more aspects of voice production

monologue technique: a technique used by actors to analyze text spoken or sung by a character

nasal pharynx: the area behind the nose and the sinus cavities

National Association of Teachers of Singing (NATS): an American organization founded to promote the interests and needs of teachers of singing

noble posture: a term used by Richard Miller to describe the best possible body stance for singing: the sternum is lifted, but not raised; the chest and upper body are poised but not tense; and the lower body is energized

obliques: internal and external muscles of the abdominal area

onset: start of phonation; attack

opera: a musical composition for voices and orchestra that is typically dramatic in nature

oral pharynx: the resonating space inside the mouth

oratorio: a musical composition for voices and orchestra that is usually based on biblical text and is not dramatically staged

oscillation: back and forth movement; in singing, movement propagated by airflow

ossification: the process of tissue hardening and turning into bone

oversinging: singing with too heavy a mechanism

overtones: complex musical tones that enhance resonance

passaggio: "passage" in Italian; the transition point from one register to another

pharynx: the resonating area above the larynx and within the mouth

phonation: production of sound by the larynx

pivot singer: in choral ensembles, a singer who can switch between different parts

plosive consonant: a consonant that is pronounced with a complete stop of airflow, followed by release

portamento: a sliding or gliding movement of the voice from one pitch to another

presto: in the context of musical composition, quick; a fast tempo

primo passaggio: the transition point between the lowest and middle registers

recovery: the final stage of the breath cycle, in which the lungs complete their recoil and the diaphragm resets

rectus abdominis: a large, flat muscle of the abdominal area

rectus sheath: a large muscle of the abdominal area

reference: in choral singing, the auditory sensation of other voices

register: a part of the voice in which all pitches share a similar quality

repertoire: the music that a singer performs

resonance: in singing, the ringing of the voice; enhanced tone

resonance tract: the area in which vocal tone resonates, from the larynx to the teeth; also known as the vocal tract

respiration: the act of breathing

secondo passaggio: the transition point between the middle and top registers

sharp: in singing, not centered and too high in pitch

sight-reading: the act of performing music while reading the notation for the first time

sight-singing: in choral singing, the act of singing a score for the first time without any previous preparation

singers' formant: a frequency range that gives singers an optimal ring in their voice

singing by sensation: the act of producing tone by sensing resonance, relying on muscle memory, and being aware of one's own voice production

slides: in singing, vocalizing between the two ends of an interval, and singing indiscriminate pitches in a sliding motion

soft palate: the rear, top area of the mouth

solfege: a system of syllables (do, re, mi, etc.) that directly relate to pitches

soprano: a voice classification for women that lies above the mezzo-soprano; or, in choral singing, the highest part for women

sostenuto: sustained

soubrette: a fach for the female singer who sings the roles of young, romantically inclined characters in opera

spinto: a classification of the soprano voice, lower than the mezzo-soprano

squillo: literally "ring"

staccato: in musical articulation, short and detached

staggered breathing: in choral singing, the practice of taking a breath within a phrase instead of before or immediately after a phrase; or, a breathing technique that allows choral singers to sustain a long phrase

sternum: the long, flat bone located at the center of the chest and attached to the clavicles (collar bones) and ribs; also known as the breastbone

straight tone: tone produced without vibrato

strohbass: a register of the male voice lying below the low register and not often used

subglottal pressure: a buildup of air below the glottis

subtext: a term used by actors to describe the unexpressed thoughts of a character; or, in singing, the underlying thoughts that motivate the sung words

suprahyoids: a group of extrinsic muscles that raise the larynx

suspension: the second stage of the breath cycle; the moment after inhalation, before the sung phrase begins

tenor: a voice classification used for men, above the baritone; or, in choral singing, the highest part for men

tenuto: a pitch held for its full value for emphasis

tessitura: a group of pitches in the same range; "texture" in Italian

thoracic cage: the ribcage, which protects the internal organs

thorax: the region of the body that extends from the neck to the diaphragm, excluding the arms

thyroarytenoid: an intrinsic muscle of the larynx

thyroid cartilage: the largest cartilage of the larynx

timbre: in singing, the quality of a tone; in acoustic science, the physical qualities of a tone, including its overtones

tone quality: the characteristics of sung tone; timbre

trachea: the airway that is fixed beneath the larynx and allows air to travel to the lungs; windpipe

transversus abdominis: the deepest of the major abdominal muscles

tremolo: what is generally thought of as a fast vibrato rate

undersinging: singing without energy in the breath or tone

vibrato: in singing, a measurable undulation of pitch and intensity

viscera: the internal organs in the chest and abdominal area

vocal cords: paired muscles within the larynx that can vibrate and produce sound; also known as the vocal folds

vocal folds: paired muscles within the larynx that can vibrate and produce sound; also known as the vocal cords

vocal fry: the lowest vocal register, with a kind of apocopated phonation not often employed in singing

vocal tract: in singing, the space between the larynx and the lips where resonance can be enhanced or modified

vocalise: a vocal exercise for singers

vocalize: to practice vocal technique in a purposeful, systematic manner; warm up

vocologist: a specialist who works with singers to habilitate the voice through study and practice

vocology: the science of vocal fitness and treatment of voice disorders

voice placement: in singing, an unscientific concept used to locationally direct students' resonance or vocal energy

voiced fricative: a consonant produced by airflow passing through a narrow mouth opening; examples include [v], [f], and [z]

vowel color: the tonal quality of a certain vowel sound

vowel modification: in singing, changing the inherent shape of a vowel by using the articulators; changing the shape of a vowel within a challenging *tessitura* for easier production of tone

vowel prescription: in choral singing, a vowel that is demonstrated by the conductor, for the ensemble, as an example

warm-up: in singing, the use of vocal exercises to prepare the voice for repertoire

wobble: in singing, a vibrato that is too slow or unsteady

Bibliography

Alderson, Richard. *Complete Handbook of Voice Training.* New York: Parker Publishing Company, 1979.

Alt, David. "Misunderstanding Breath Support for Singers." *Choral Journal* 30 (1990): 33–35.

Appleman, D. Ralph. *The Science of Vocal Pedagogy: Theory and Application.* Bloomington: Indiana University Press, 1967.

Baken, R. J. "The Aged Voice: A New Hypothesis." *Journal of Voice* 19 (2005): 317–25.

Bennett, Roy C. *The Choral Singer's Handbook.* Melville, NY: Belwin-Mills Publishing, 1977.

Blades-Zeller, Elizabeth. *A Spectrum of Voices: Prominent American Voice Teachers Discuss the Teaching of Singing.* Lanham, MD: The Scarecrow Press, 2002.

Boone, Daniel R. "The Three Ages of Voice: The Singing/Acting Voice in the Mature Adult." *Journal of Voice* 11 (1997): 161–64.

Brown, W. S. Jr., Richard J. Morris, and John F. Michel. "Vocal Jitter and Fundamental Frequency Characteristics in Aged, Female Professional Singers." *Journal of Voice* 4 (1990): 135–41.

Bunch, Meribeth. *Dynamics of the Singing Voice.* Vienna, Austria: Springer-Verlag, 1982.

Christiansen, Olaf C. "Solo and Ensemble Singing." *The NATS Bulletin* 21 (February 1965): 16–17, 40.

Cleall, Charles. *Voice Production in Choral Technique.* London: Novello and Company, 1970.

Cleveland, Thomas F. "A Comparison of Breath Management Strategies in Classical and Nonclassical Singers: Part 2." *Journal of Singing* 55 (1998): 45–46.

Coleman, Robert F. "Performance Demands and the Performer's Vocal Capabilities." *Journal of Voice* 1 (1987): 209–16.

Colson, Greta. *Voice Production and Speech*. London: Museum Press, 1964.

Cox, Dennis K. "Vocalization: A Primary Vehicle for the Enhancement of the Physical, Mental and Emotional Factors in Choral Tone." *Choral Journal* 30 (1989): 17–19.

Critchley, MacDonald, and R. A. Henson. *Music and the Brain: Studies in the Neurology of Music*. London: William Heinemann Medical Books, 1977.

David, Marilee. *The New Voice Pedagogy*. London: The Scarecrow Press, 1995.

DeBroder, Gordon. "Vocal Hints for Students." *The NATS Journal* 45 (1989): 13.

Delattre, Pierre, and John Howie. "An Experimental Study of the Effect of Pitch on the Intelligibility of Vowels." *The NATS Bulletin* 18 (1962): 6–9.

Dicke, Martin P. "Non-Vibrato Singing: An Historical Feature of the Performance of Early Music or a 20th Century Performance Practice Fad?" (unpublished research paper, 1999).

Dickson, John. "Musical Pride and Textual Prejudice: The Expressivity of Language in Choral Music." *Choral Journal* 36 (1993): 9–11.

Diercks, Louis H., and E. Milton Boone. "The Individual in the Choral Situation." *The NATS Bulletin* 17 (May 1961): 6–10.

Dornemann, Joan. *Complete Preparation: A Guide to Auditioning for Opera*. New York: Excalibur Publishing, 1994.

Doscher, Barbara M. *The Functional Unity of the Singing Voice*. 2nd ed. London: The Scarecrow Press, 1994.

———. "Teaching Singing." *The Quarterly Journal of Music Teaching and Learning* 3 (1992): 61–66.

———. "Exploring the Whys of Intonation Problems." *Choral Journal* 32 (1991): 25–33.

Edwin, Robert. "The Good, the Bad, and the Ugly: Singing Teacher–Choral Director Relationships." *Journal of Singing* 57 (2001): 53–54.

Ehmann, Wilhelm, and Frauke Haasemann. *Voice Building for Choirs*. Englewood Cliffs, NJ: Prentice Hall, 1988.

Elliot, Ninn, Johan Sundberg, and Patricia Gramming. "Physiological Aspects of a Vocal Exercise." *Journal of Voice* 11 (1997): 171–76.

Feder, Robert J. "Vocal Health: A View from the Medical Profession." *Choral Journal* 30 (1990): 23–25.

Foster, Walter C. *Singing Redefined: A Conceptual Approach to Singing*. Huntsville, TX: Recital Publications, 1998.

Garcia, Manuel, II. *The Art of Singing, Part I*. Boston: Ditson, c. 1855.

Garretson, Robert. *Conducting Choral Music*. Upper Saddle River, NJ: Prentice Hall, 1998.

Goodwin, Allen W. "An Acoustical Study of Individual Voices in Choral Blend." *Journal of Research in Singing and Applied Vocal Pedagogy* 13 (1989): 25–34.

Gregg, Jean Westerman. "On Vibrato." *The NATS Journal* 94 (1994): 45–47.

———. "On Voice and Age." *The NATS Journal* 47 (1990): 32–35.

Gruson, Linda M. "Rehearsal Skill and Musical Competence: Does Practice Make Perfect?" In *Generative Processes in Music: The Psychology of Performance, Improvisation and Composition*, edited by John A. Sloboda, 91–112. Oxford: Clarendon Press, 1988.

Haasemann, Frauke, and James M. Jordan. *Group Vocal Technique*. Chapel Hill, NC: Hinshaw Music, 1991.

Hemsley, Thomas. *Singing and Imagination: A Human Approach to a Great Musical Tradition*. Oxford, UK: Oxford University Press, 1998.

Ingham, Paul E., and Alan L. Keaton. "Vocal Nodules and the Choral Conductor." *Choral Journal* 24 (1983): 5–6.

Jordan, James M. "False Blend: A Vocal Pedagogy Problem for the Choral Conductor." *Choral Journal* 24 (1984): 25–27.

Judson, Lyman S. V., and Andrew Thomas Weaver. *Voice Science*. New York: Appleton-Century-Crofts, 1965.

Kelly, Terence. "The Authenticity of Continuous Vocal Vibrato: An Empirical and Historical Examination." *The NATS Journal* 51 (1995): 3–6.

Lamb, Gordon H. *Choral Techniques*. Dubuque, IA: Wm. C. Brown Company, 1974.

Lawrence, Van, ed. *Transcripts of the Sixth Symposium, Care of the Professional Voice*. New York: The Voice Foundation, 1977.

Leyerle, William D. *Vocal Development through Organic Imagery*. Genesco: State University of New York, 1977.

Lloyd, Thomas. "Am I Being Followed? Finding the Elusive Connection between Conductor and Ensemble." *Choral Journal* 36 (1996): 23–27.

Marek, Dan H. *Singing: The First Art*. Lanham, MD: The Scarecrow Press, 2007.

McKinney, James C. *The Diagnosis and Correction of Vocal Faults*. Nashville, TN: Genevox Music Group, 1994.

Miller, Richard. "Acknowledging an Indebtedness." *Choral Journal* 49 (2008): 16–22.

———. *Solutions for Singers: Tools for Performers and Teachers*. Oxford, UK: Oxford University Press, 2004.

———. *National Schools of Singing: English, French, German and Italian Techniques of Singing Revisited*. London: The Scarecrow Press, 1997.

———. *On the Art of Singing*. New York: Oxford University Press, 1996.

———. *The Structure of Singing: System and Art in Vocal Technique*. New York: Schirmer Books, 1996.

———. "The Solo Singer in the Choral Ensemble." *Choral Journal* 36 (1995): 31–36.

Moore, Dale. "A Plea for Dialogue." *The NATS Journal* (January–February 1990): 3–5.

Morgan, Jan. "The Solo Voice and Choral Singing." *Choral Journal* 2 (1970): 11–12.

Neuen, Donald. "The Young Soprano Voice." *American Choral Review* 33 (1991): 40–42.

O'Toole, Patricia. "I Sing in a Choir But I Have No Voice!" *The Quarterly Journal of Music Teaching and Learning* (Winter–Spring 1993): 65–76.

Palmer, Anthony J. "Treating the Choral Singer as a Person." *Choral Journal* 22 (1981): 29–32.

Peterson, Barry W., and Frances J. Richmond. *Control of Head Movement*. New York: Oxford University Press, 1988.

Peterson, Paul W. "Problems of Choral Blend." *The NATS Bulletin* 8 (1952): 2.

Pfautsch, Lloyd. "The Choral Conductor and the Rehearsal." In *Choral Conducting Symposium*, edited by Harold A. Decker and Julius Herford, 69–110. Englewood Cliffs, NJ: Prentice Hall, 1988.

Proctor, Donald F. *Breathing, Speech and Song*. New York: Springer-Verlag, 1980.

Rasch, Rudolf A., and John A. Sloboda, eds. *Timing and Synchronization in Ensemble Performance, Improvisation and Composition*. Oxford, UK: Oxford Science Publications, 1988.

Rayapati, Sangeetha. "Teaching Reaches Out: Class Voice and the Aging Singer." *Journal of Singing* 64 (2008): 543–50.

Reid, Katherine L. P., Pamela Davis, Jennifer Oates, Densil Cabrera, Sten Ternström, Michael Black, and Janice Chapman. "The Acoustic Characteristics of Professional Opera Singers Performing in Chorus Versus Solo Mode." *Journal of Voice* 21 (2007): 35–45.

Robinson, Ray, and Allen Winold. *The Choral Experience: Literature, Materials, and Methods*. Prospect Heights, IL: Waveland Press, 1976.

Roe, Paul F. *Choral Music Education*. Prospect Heights, IL: Waveland Press, 1983.

Sabol, Julianna Wrycza, Linda Lee, and Joseph C. Stemple. "The Value of Vocal Function Exercises in the Practice Regimen of Singers." *Journal of Voice* 9 (1995): 27–34.

Sataloff, Robert T. "Arts Medicine: An Overview for Choir Conductors." *Choral Journal* 49 (2008): 25–33.

———. "Vocal Aging and Its Medical Implications: What Singing Teachers Should Know, Part I." *Journal of Singing* 57 (2000): 29–31.

Sataloff, Robert T., Deborah C. Rosen, Mary Hawkshaw, Joseph R. Spiegel, et al. "The Three Ages of Voice: The Aging Adult Voice." *Journal of Voice* 11 (1997): 156–60

Schenbeck, Lyn. "Finding the Poet's Voice: Strategies for Collective Interpretation of Choral Text." *Choral Journal* 40 (2000): 9–16.

Smith, Brenda, and Robert T. Sataloff. *Choral Pedagogy*. San Diego: Singular Publishing Group, 2000.

Stanley, Douglas. *The Science of Voice*. New York: Carl Fischer, 1939.

Sundberg, Johan. *The Science of Musical Sounds*. New York: Academic Press, 1991.

———. *The Science of the Singing Voice*. Dekalb: Northern Illinois University Press, 1987.

———. *Research Aspects on Singing*. Stockholm: Royal Swedish Academy of Music, 1981.

———. "To Perceive One's Own Voice and Another Person's Voice." In *Research Aspects on Singing*, edited by Johan Sundberg, 80–96. Stockholm: Royal Swedish Academy of Music, 1981.

Sundberg, Johan, R. Leanderson, C. von Euler, and E. Knutsson. "Influence of Body Posture and Lung Volume on Subglottal Pressure Control during Singing." *Journal of Voice* 5 (1991): 283–91.

Sundberg, Johan, Anders Friberg, and Lars Fryden. "Common Secrets of Musicians and Listeners: An Analysis by Synthesis Study of Musical Performance." In *Representing Musical Structure*, edited by Peter Howell, Robert West, and Ian Cross, 71–91. London: Academic Press, 1991.

Swan, Howard. "The Development of a Choral Instrument." In *Choral Conducting Symposium*, edited by Harold A. Decker and Julius Herford, 7–68. Englewood Cliffs, NJ: Prentice Hall, 1988.

Ternström, Sten. "Hearing Myself with Others: Sound Levels in Choral Performance Measured with Separation of One's Own Voice from the Rest of the Choir." *Journal of Voice* 8 (1994): 293–302.

———. "Physical and Acoustic Factors That Interact with the Singer to Produce the Choral Sound." *Journal of Voice* 5 (1991): 128–42.

Thurman, Leon. "Voice Health and Choral Singing: When Voice Classifications Limit Singing Ability." *Choral Journal* 28 (1988): 25–33.

———. "Putting Horses Before Carts: When Choral Singing Hurts Voices." *Choral Journal* 23 (1983): 23–28.

Thurman, Leon, and Carol Litzke. "Dealing with Vocal Distress on the Day of a Concert." *Choral Journal* 35 (1994): 29–32.

Titze, Ingo. "Getting the Most from the Vocal Instrument in a Choral Setting." *Choral Journal* 49 (2008): 34–41.

———. "Choir Warm-Ups: How Effective Are They?" *The NATS Journal* 56 (2000): 31–32.

———. "Edward Byrom's Reply to 'Choir Warm-Ups: How Effective Are They?'" *Journal of Singing* 58 (September–October 2001): 57–58.

———. "Keeping It Moist." *The NATS Journal* 51 (1995): 39–40.

———. *Principles of Voice Production.* Englewood Cliffs, NJ: Prentice Hall, 1994.

———. "A Few Thoughts about Longevity in Singing." *The NATS Journal* 50 (1994): 35–36.

———. "Critical Periods of Vocal Change: Advanced Age." *The NATS Journal* 49 (1993): 27.

———. "The Physiologic Absurdity of Choir Arrangements." *The NATS Journal* 46 (1989): 18.

Titze, Ingo, and Ronald C. Scherer, eds. *Vocal Fold Physiology: Biomechanics, Acoustics and Phonatory Control.* Denver: The Denver Center for the Performing Arts, 1983.

Tonkinson, Steven. "The Lombard Effect in Choral Singing." *Journal of Voice* 8 (1994): 24–29.

Vennard, William. *Singing: The Mechanism and the Technic*. New York: Carl Fischer, 1968.

Von Ellefson, Randi. "An Opera Soloist Reflects on Choral Singing: An Interview with Thomas Hampson." *Choral Journal* 37 (1996): 37–39.

Ware, Clifton. *Basics of Vocal Pedagogy: The Foundations and Process of Singing*. Boston: McGraw-Hill, 1998.

Woodruff, Harvey L. "The Choral Conductor." *The NATS Bulletin* 10 (1953): 14–22.

Wrolstad, James Luther. "The Effect of Choral Singing on the Developing Solo Voice." Master's Thesis, California State University, Fullerton, 1979.

Index

~

About the Author

Margaret Olson is currently assistant professor and coordinator of vocal studies at Morgan State University in Baltimore, Maryland, home of the world-renowned Morgan State Choir.

She has performed frequently in the United States as a solo and chamber musician. Her opera roles include Miss Wordsworth in *Albert Herring*, Belinda in *Dido and Aeneas*, and the Heroine in the world premiere of *Fatal Song* with the University of Maryland Opera Studio. Recent performances include a Christmas recital at the White House and State Department in Washington, DC, with tenor Lawrence Reppert and pianist Patrick O'Donnell; several recitals of "20th Century Songs in English," featuring music of Quilter, Britten, Duke, Hundley, and Porter, at various venues in Washington, DC, and Maryland with pianist James Lee III; and chamber music recitals at Towson State University, Anne Arundel Community College, Morgan State University, and the Walters Art Museum in Baltimore, Maryland.

She has held teaching positions with the Washington National Opera Institute, Georgetown University, the University of Tennessee, Iowa Wesleyan College, and Peabody Conservatory, and has been a guest lecturer with the Handel Choir of Baltimore and the Baltimore School for the Arts, among others.

Her directing credits include *Big River* at the University of Tennessee, *A Game of Chance* at the University of Iowa, and *Abduction from the Seraglio* (as assistant director) at Indiana University, Bloomington. She was awarded the Boris Goldovsky Opera Directing Internship with the Crittenden Opera

Workshop, and has studied directing with Sally Stunkel, Stephano Vizioli (La Scala Opera), and Richard Crittenden.

She participated in the intern program of the National Association of Teachers of Singing, class of 2001, and has also served that organization as a singer, scholar, and judge. She currently serves on its Strategic Planning Committee.

Her articles have been published in *Choral Journal* and the *Journal of Singing*. She worked as a teaching artist for the Cathedral Choral Society and Choral Arts Society in Washington, DC, and the Wolf Trap Education Foundation.

Her research interests include American song, voice science and pedagogy, collaborative chamber music performance, and, of course, the solo singer in the choral setting.

Her students have performed with the Philadelphia and Baltimore Opera Companies, and have won various regional competitions and the NATS student auditions at the state and regional levels. Her students have also been cast in national Broadway tours and admitted to graduate programs.

She holds the following degrees: D.M.A., University of Iowa (voice performance and pedagogy); M.M., University of Maryland, College Park (opera performance); and B.M., University of North Carolina, Greensboro (voice performance).